THIS BOOK BELONGS TO

....

CONTENTS

*IT'S NOT A PODCAST...

... But it was going to be. The plan was to record beautiful Dartmoor sounds, then use the power of language to paint a picture of my surroundings in your mind. It became apparent, though, pretty soon, that I didn't have the verbal skills to do that, and that it would be much nicer if you could just see what I was waffling on about. So I bought a GoPro camera and got filming.

But I'd already set up the email, twitter account, and YouTube channel, and didn't want to go through all that faff again, so decided to just keep the name and make it a relentlessly recurring joke instead.

I have, by now, certainly spent more time explaining this to people than it would have taken to change the email address.

Also, who knows how many viewers I've lost due to people thinking it's another insufferable podcast rather than a series of cheeky little videos that they might enjoy. I try not to think about it.

Still – I got an irritating catchphrase out of it.

ABOUT THIS BOOK

Thank you, by the way, for buying this incredibly niche item!

I don't think you'll regret it.

If I had any hopes or dreams of making any money out of the podcast*, I'd be setting up a Patreon, shilling terrible wild camping gadgets, and constantly nagging you all to 'like and subscribe'. No – that wouldn't do at all.

If you like the podcast*, then you'll like this book. It's a good deal for everyone – I get a few bob to pump back into making better and better episodes, and you get something you'll genuinely enjoy.

Here's what you'll get:

- **A review of each episode.** I never watch the episodes back once they've been unleashed on the world, so that should be fun. I'll try and explain the embarrassing decisions I made in the production of each episode, and burden you with my additional thoughts and regrets.
- **The script for each episode.** These are usually cut down a bit in the editing, so there are some extra nuggets in there for you die-hard fans (by which I mean people who really like my work, not people who love the series of action films starring Bruce Willis).
- **Easter eggs and bonus nuggets for each episode!** I like to put a few silly little jokes and references into most episodes that never

get noticed, so here's my chance to share them and show everyone how clever I am.

- **Facts and Puzzles!** The Dartmoor Podcast* is here to entertain, but also to educate, so enjoy some extra factual gubbins and retro puzzles. Despite the puzzles being conceived as a joke about the aesthetic of retro annuals, I ended up trying to make them genuinely challenging. They took a lot longer than I thought they would.
- **Pictures!** Why not? Let's justify the price of this book with some photos for you.
- **Appendices!** I've scanned in some pages from my 'serial killer notebook', so you can see the raw material that goes into making the damn thing. I've no idea if this will be of interest to anyone.
- And I'll even slip in a link to **bonus material** that isn't publicly available on YouTube (don't tell anyone!). Sadly, I didn't keep a lot of stuff from 2022 as I needed space on my computer, but this should get better in future annuals!

Thank you once again for your purchase. I'm sorry you had to buy it off an evil corporation, but, honestly, would any proper publisher touch this nonsense with a barge pole? I doubt it.

THE DARTMOOR PODCAST EPISODE ONE

01/04/2022

SEARCH FOR THE NUTCRACKER

NOOOO! WHYYYYY!

EPISODE REVIEW

Ah! The naivety! I haven't got a nice font, haven't colour-corrected any footage, it's wobbly, sounds weird, and half of it is out of focus.

Actually, though, this isn't a bad first attempt, is it? Probably because I spent an absurd amount of time thinking about it compared to other episodes. There are two (mercifully deleted) previous attempts at it – one purely audio version, and one where I try and vlog like all the other YouTubers.

Still, the foundations are there, right? The little guitar jingle, the weird selfie-stick camera angle, the pretentious lens-flare shots. There's even a little tea-making montage. Oh, and a few nice narrative twists and turns.

I like the joke where the music stops abruptly and I run back to get the camera. I'm proud that I have stuck to my promise to never do those 'walk away' shots – whenever I see one, I can literally think of nothing except "they're going to have to walk back and get that" and it takes me right out of the experience.

All of this is only minorly undermined by the fact that the boulder I found down in the woods clearly isn't the Christening Bowl – it's too far away and in the wrong direction. I think I have found the real one since, though!

SCRIPT

When most people think of Dartmoor, they think of craggy tors atop barren hills under an imposing sky. But here, on the East side of the moors, everything's a little bit softer, a little bit gentler, a little bit greener (or, at least it would be if it weren't February), and a little bit friendlier. I always think of it as the 'Hobbiton' side of the moors.

Welcome to the Dartmoor Podcast, by the way! I'm George, and I love nothing better than wandering about on the moors searching for a good story. And today, I've got a cracker!

I'm walking up Lustleigh Cleave - a beautiful, steep-sided valley where the sound of the River Bovey is never far away. And roaming through the woods here, it would be easy to think that this forest has stood here since ancient times. But in reality, even just a hundred years ago, this was all open farmland. And here and there, hidden amongst the undergrowth are the ruins of stone walls, and farmhouses, and wells.

But that's not what I'm exploring today. I'm looking for a mysterious *natural* feature - a logan stone.

A logan stone is created when a stack of rock is eroded in such a way that a large boulder is left balanced on a tiny nub. And what makes this fun, is that it is balanced so precisely on its little granite crystal, that it can be rocked from side to side by hand - a 'rocking rock'.

Now, some people believe that these stones were used thousands of years ago by the druids in magic rituals, and it is quite appealing to imagine some druidic shaman displaying his powers, and wowing his tribe by moving a massive boulder with just a touch of his finger...

But there's literally no evidence for that!

Nonetheless, I thought it would be an exciting little adventure to hunt down this logan stone. Because who wouldn't want to shamanically wobble a rock in their spare time?

Now, looking at the map, you can see that Lustleigh Cleave is this green area following the River Bovey along the Eastern fringe of the moor, and high on the ridge above the cleave is Sharpitor. And just beneath Sharpitor - the word 'Nutcrackers'. You see, one of the uses of a precariously balanced, multi-ton slab of granite is that it can be used to crack nuts, and it would be remiss of me not to have brought a pocket full of walnuts for exactly this purpose.

However, as you can see, the map doesn't show exactly where this logan stone is, only giving a rather general area. And Sharpitor, I know, is a rambling, tumble-down maze of boulders. So trying to locate the one rock that sways, amongst all the other scattered rocks could be like looking for a needle in a haystack. All part of the adventure, right?

Well... it turns out that the imprecision of the map might actually be the least of my problems.

Because on Sunday the 7th May 1950, the residents of Lustleigh woke up to find the Nutcracker gone.

Several tons of solid granite sent tumbling off the side of the Cleave and crashing into the valley below.

Well, a little dive into the local newspaper archives shows that this caused quite a stir! Here is what was appeared in the Western Morning News on May the 11th:

Lustleigh Cleave's famous 'Nutcracker Rock' – a 10 ton granite logan-stone so precisely balanced by Nature that once it could be gently rocked by hand, has been dislodged by vandals and now lies 40ft below its granite pedestal...

Mr F. Amery, clerk to the parish council said yesterday "The village feels outraged by this wanton act. The rock has been a showpiece for the cleave and could be seen for miles".

A Mrs Saville of the village said "We are extremely indignant that some vandals should have done this. The rock must have been in its position since prehistoric times and it is a shame it should be destroyed now. I can only hope the culprits will be found and punished!"

(I'm allowed to do that voice – I'm from Devon).

There was even a witness to the crime, with a Miss Cook, who lived nearby (at Nutcracker Cottage, no less), reporting this to the Western Times on May the 19th:

"I saw two men with crowbars on Saturday night, and they told me they were going to push a boulder over. I was on the way back to my cottage when I heard a crash. Had I known they intended to push over the Nutcracker, I would have done my best to stop them."

Yes, it turns out that a couple of Lustleigh lads, no doubt after a few pints down the pub on a Saturday night, decided it would be funny to lever the rock off the top of the cliff. And despite the anger of the locals, the police weren't interested.

Is this the end of the tale? Have my plans to wobble the Nutcracker been dashed by a pair of drunks from the 1950s? Not so fast!

Because somehow, the Lustleigh council managed to persuade the *army* that it would be a good use of the military's time to come and replace the stone.

Back to the papers!

"War office approval has been given to the Coast Artillery School, the Royal Citadel, Plymouth for what will be known as 'Operation Nutcracker'"

This would involve a convoy of lorries and heavy winching equipment navigating the narrow Dartmoor roads, and making camp near Lustleigh before attempting to lift the stone. This operation was led by the wonderfully named Captain Juniper, who said it would be a *'practical job of work in training'*, and that he was sure of succeeding *'as long as it didn't rain...'*

And despite it being summer, it *was* Dartmoor, so it rained - for five days straight. And when the soldiers came to winch the rock, on Monday the 19th of June a cable snapped and the stone *"slid over the ledge, and thundered 100 feet to the bottom of the valley"*.

Despite this cataclysmic failure, it's interesting to note that Captain Juniper was still able to look on the bright side, saying *"the men have had first-rate experience", and that the hospitality of the locals was so superb that they were "reluctant to leave".*

So, why am I stomping across Dartmoor with a pocket full of walnuts?

Well, there is a final twist in the tale.

On the map, it doesn't say 'Nutcracker', it says '*Nutcrackers*'. Apparently Sharpitor was home to a trio of logan stones: the Nutcracker, the Christening Bowl, and the Sofa.

The vandals didn't lever all three off, did they?

There was even a short clipping in the Western Morning News at the time, where a Lustleigh resident - Mrs Mary Smale - claimed that it was actually the Christening Bowl which had been pushed over the cliff and that the Nutcracker was still standing. And to prove it, she presented a handful of cracked hazelnut shells.

The mission is back on!

So, despite a rather circuitous route, I'm back where I started - looking for the Nutcracker among a huge jumble of rocks. Not an easy task...

Luckily, I have an ace up my sleeve! This wonderful old black and white photo of someone giving the Nutcracker a little wobble. So, in theory, I should be able to use this picture to locate the correct place, and, if Mary Smale was correct, to find the Nutcracker.

The first thing you'll notice is how all these trees have sprung up in the last 70 years! I think my best bet will be to try and match up the hills in the background of the photo to get me in the right area (I think this little blur in the middle is Houndtor, so I need to move further round from here).

It's a good job I'm doing this in February, as I imagine it would be nearly impossible if the leaves were out on the trees now.

Loads of interesting little nooks and crannies up here! And some nice views where it opens out a bit.

After a bit of scrabbling about, I've finally find the place I'm looking for... and the Nutcracker remains! This distinctive rounded boulder on the nose of this outcrop.

And Mary Smale was right. This other photo shows that the Christening Bowl is the one that was dislodged. It must have made quite a crash as it fell, as it was a huge rock - much bigger than the Nutcracker.

Only one thing left to do...

NOooo! Whyyy!

Oh well, more than one way to crack a nut.

Was Mary Smale having us on? Or did the Nutcracker become defunct in the time since?

I have to say I'm disappointed that the Nutcracker has lost its wobble. But sitting up here on the site of the Christening Bowl, I've at least found a spectacular view.

And if I was to take some of Captain Juniper's optimism, I suppose I could say that the adventure still lies ahead of me! Does anyone know of a functioning Dartmoor logan stone I could find for a future mission?

As a little bonus, I've had a search down in the valley below Sharpitor, and think I've found what remains of the Christening Bowl. I can't be sure, but this rock just looks out of place, and you can see how this tree has grown around it. Also, there are some grooves on the rock which look like they could have been caused by a thick metal cable grinding against it. And this, about 50 metres away, could be the other half, perhaps. Those grooves again, look. In fact, I saw some of those same grooves on the Nutcracker, so maybe the army not only dropped the Christening Bowl, but unbalanced the Nutcracker in the process!

Thank you for listening. I hope you found some of it interesting, anyway! See you next time! Bye bye!

EASTER EGGS, GOOFS, AND EXTRA NUGGETS

- The 'theme music' to The Dartmoor Podcast* is me playing a song called *Build Another Band* by Bert Jansch. I've always loved this song since I heard the amazing version which opens the live album *The River Sessions*.
- The nice font isn't here yet, but at least it's the right colour. I made an early decision to make my 'brand' colour yellow because it's the colour of the Dartmoor gorse.
- The shot of me posing on the rock flicks briefly to the painting *Wanderer Above the Sea of Fog* by Caspar David Friedrich, a Romantic painter who I like to think captures the spirit of the Dartmoor Podcast*. Later, above a foggy Lustleigh Cleave, my brother would catch a nice photo of me recreating this pose which has since become my logo.
- The Dartmoor Podcast* letterbox can be found near the spot where I do the *Wanderer Above the Sea of Fog* pose, and my Geocache can be found behind the boulder down in the woods. More on this later...
- I really like that I published my first episode on April Fools' Day. It seems appropriate, somehow.

LUSTLEIGH CLEAVE LOCATIONS

Lustleigh Cleave gets a disproportionate amount of representation on the podcast*, as it's the easiest place for me to get to. Like everywhere on Dartmoor, it has some pretty strange place names. Can you guess what features these pictures relate to?

THE DARTMOOR PODCAST EPISODE TWO

24/04/2022

THE LESSER-SPOTTED WOODPECKER

LSW, AS THE COOL BIRDERS CALL IT (PHOTO: KAYLEIGH WALL)

EPISODE REVIEW

The worst episode by far. Still, I shan't be too hard on myself as I was just learning what would and wouldn't work. Also, it's mercifully short.

This episode does have the first ever use of the 'book slam', though, which has become a Dartmoor Podcast* staple. I apologise if it's scared the life out of you at any point when you've dozed off while listening to an episode.

In hindsight, this episode would've been much better to save for when I had a fancy camera that could zoom in. Luckily, I was able to chuck in a few photos by my sister-in-law so you can actually see what the bird looks like.

Overall, this lacks the humour and narrative that a proper Dartmoor Podcast* episode needs. But it's quite nice and relaxing, I suppose… Other than those book slams!

SCRIPT

Lesser Spotted Woodpecker, Lesser Spotted Woodpecker, Lesser Spotted Woodpecker, not a Great Spotted Woodpecker, Lesser Spotted Woodpecker.

It's mid-March, and spring is just beginning to poke its head out here on the moors. What a beautiful time to be roaming about on a new mission for The Dartmoor Podcast.

Today, I'm looking for one of my favourite birds (top five, at least): the rare and secretive Lesser Spotted Woodpecker. To find one of these mysterious little buggers is no easy task, but, if everything aligns as I hope it will, we'll get a glimpse of one today!

I should mention at this point, that I'm not packing any serious optical equipment, so if you're expecting some stunning, Attenboroughesque, documentary shots of these shy little birds, you're going to be disappointed. But if you want to know how to find a little woodpecker of your own, then you have come to exactly the right place.

I'll start by explaining why the Lesser Spotted Woodpecker is such a tricky bird to find.

Firstly, they're just rare. There just aren't very many of them, and certainly not many on Dartmoor. This wonderful tome shows that they could only be found in a handful of places back 2013, and I can assure you with near certainty that there are even fewer now.

(Sigh) That's a depressing map, isn't it.

Secondly, they are sneaky. The Lesser-Spot (as all the cool birders call them) is one of nature's introverts. They range over a large area, like to stay high-up amongst the leaves, and don't make a lot of noise.

Thirdly, the layman will easily confuse them with their common cousin the Great Spotted Woodpecker. I expect most people would open their bird book, take a look at the pictures of these two and go 'nope – not telling those apart'!

But there is one key difference that perhaps doesn't come across in these pictures, and it is also the fourth reason why the Lesser Spotted Woodpecker is hard to see. They're tiny!

You see, the name 'Lesser Spotted' doesn't mean that it is seen less often (though, in this case, that is certainly true), nor does it mean that it has fewer spots. It means it is much smaller - The *Lesser* Spottedwoodpecker.

The Great Spotted Woodpecker is a big, bold chap, about the size of a Blackbird, whereas the Lesser Spotted, is only about the size of a Sparrow.

So how do we go about finding a tiny, shy, rare bird that hides in the treetops in large areas of woodland?

Well, luckily for us, there is a short window, right at this time of year, when the Lesser Spot lets its guard down and decides to call and drum to attract a mate. And serendipitously, this is also the time of year when the leaves aren't quite out on the trees, so you can actually see them!

And even then, there's no guarantee of success. But that's the beauty of birding, right?

To give myself the best chance of finding one of these little darlings, I will need to get out early, and the best way to do this is certainly by camping out. Can there be anything better than waking up on Dartmoor on a cold spring morning?

Listen! That's a drumming woodpecker. What a wonderful sound, echoing up from the valley in the morning air! But that's a Great Spotted Woodpecker – a short burst of drumming, but loud and confident. The Lesser Spotted creates a softer but more sustained rattle. Hopefully I can demonstrate that in a bit!

Now, I can't tell you the exact location here, because the Lesser Spotted Woodpecker is protected. I'm not sure that egg collectors are much of a thing these days, but over-zealous photographers certainly are. A few years ago, I was taking a spring walk through the woods near here and heard a Lesser Spotted Woodpecker calling from near the path up ahead. When I rushed forward to try and catch a glimpse, I found a bloke playing Woodpecker calls on his phone, trying to lure them in for photo!

Please try and avoid unnecessarily disturbing these birds if you do find them.

Now it's a case of waiting and listening. I've got my ear open for a shrill little laughing call or some quiet drumming.

There!

Listen. There's that drumming. Softer but longer than the Great Spot's.

The GoPro doesn't really do it justice, but those were some of the best views of these woodpeckers I've ever had - a pair of them, drumming, calling, chasing each other around. It looks like there could be some baby woodpeckers on the way. Fingers crossed.

Last year, at this same place, we got some photos, too. Almost certainly the same bird am watching today.

And that's all there is to it! I highly recommend scheduling a Lesser Spotted Woodpecker pilgrimage into your diary for early March next year. You won't regret it.

See you next time!

EASTER EGGS, GOOFS, AND EXTRA NUGGETS

- Good news! I actually think Lesser Spotted Woodpecker numbers on Dartmoor have increased in the last couple of years since filming this episode. I certainly seem to bump into them more regularly. I'm taking full credit.
- I say that the location is secret, but in reality, it is the one place that everyone who follows any kind of birding site knows they can see a Lesser Spotted Woodpecker. You want to know? Ah, go on then, seeing as you bought my book - it's by the old reservoir at the top of Yarner Woods.
- I've had that old bird book with the detached cover since I was about eight. You can tell it's well-loved!

DARTMOOR BIRDS CROSSWORD

Across:

4. Underwater songbird (6)
6. Not a Chiff-Chaff (6,7)
8. 'Ghost of the Forest' (7)
10. 'Goat Sucker' (8)
12. 'Ossifrage' (11)
13. Tiny troglodyte (4)
14. Birding obsessive (8)
15. Pied, or Spotted? (10)
17. Tourist eagle (7)

Down:

1. Woodpecker sound (8)
2. Tree, or Meadow? (5)
3. Cover up my swears (8)
4. Breed in blanket bogs (6)
5. Call 'The Dartmoor Podcast'! (10)
7. Seen on Halloween 2022 (4,3)
9. 'White Arse' (8)
11. Just two pairs left on Dartmoor (6)
16. Raven, Jay, Jackdaw etc. (6)

THE DARTMOOR PODCAST EPISODE THREE

10/05/2022

DAWN CHORUS

&

SPRING GREENS

BUMBLING AMONG THE BLUEBELLS

EPISODE REVIEW

Still learning! This has a bit of the humour that was missing from episode two, but plenty of completely new faults, too.

For starters, it sounds dreadful – all echoey and harsh. This is due to me not realising that I got a nice 'soft' sound on the first two episodes by recording them in front of some drawn curtains.

This is the episode where I ditched the idea of my face remaining hidden throughout - a shame, as I think that would have been a nice bit of mystery, even though it would have got tricky later on. Not sure you all needed to see my flabby white belly at the start of this episode, though!

The use of the bird names popping up as they sing is quite a good idea. I especially like them being in the right colours. However, this is another example of something that would be much better if you could see the birds singing rather than a static backshot of some trees. Still, it's something I might come back to now I've got a few more filming skills (and a nicer camera).

The twice-foreshadowed ending with the badger is a nice touch. I wonder how many people watched far enough to see it!

SCRIPT

Welcome back to the Dartmoor Podcast!

It's the last day of April, and spring is in full swing. The flowers are blooming, the birds are singing, and the weather's heating up...

Well, maybe not quite warm enough for that yet.

Let's focus on the first two - the flowers and the birds.

My plan today is to camp out, wake up before the sun, and use my fancy stereo microphone to capture the sounds of the dawn chorus on Mayday... which is also, I am informed, 'international dawn chorus day'.

The reason, of course, that May is such a good time of year for the dawn chorus, is that our nesting birds are in full voice - singing their hearts out to defend their territory or attract a mate. And as an added bonus, at this time of year, some birds have flown to Dartmoor from all the way south of the equator to add their voices to the choir.

Later in this video, I'll be showing you how to identify some of Dartmoor's birdlife by their songs. I'll also upload a version of the dawn chorus without me waffling all over it, so those of you who'd prefer to just relax to some forest bird sounds can do so without me ruining it. The links is in the description.

But before we get to that, I'm going to pick some wild greens for my dinner.

Here's an easy one – Primrose! All wild plants haven't been cultivated for flavour, like our shop-bought greens, so get quite bitter once they grow older. For the best taste with any wild green, pick the smallest, palest leaves.

Dandelion. These have a bitter, rocket-y sort of taste. An old name for them was 'piss-a-bed'. I'm not sure how much I'd have to eat before I wet myself, but I'm going to pick sparingly and avoid finding out.

This is Hogweed – possibly my favourite wild edible, and one which is abundant along Dartmoor's roads and tracks at this time of year. Note the big distinctively shaped leaves and hairy purplish stem. Once you find some, have a rummage around the base and pick the unopened shoots for a yummy little 'Hog Asparagus' spear. They have a pleasant, mild, slightly cardamon-y taste.

Disclaimer - foraging for edible plants *is* an exact science. Hogweed has an invasive evil cousin called Giant Hogweed which won't just poison you, but will melt your skin off with its corrosive sap. Make sure you know what you're picking.

This pretty little pink-flowered weed with red stems and frilly leaves is Herb Robert. I find it a good coriander substitute. Strong tasting, so use sparingly.

My big disappointment is not finding any Wild Garlic today, but this is the next best thing. 'Jack-By-The Hedge'. It grows in distinctive tall towers, with distinctive clusters of with flowers and has distinctive heart-shaped, pale green, glossy leaves. It is commonly called Garlic Mustard, and tastes as you'd expect with such a name.

This is Pennywort, often found growing out of all sorts of rocks and tors up here on the moor. It can't really be confused with anything else, and the round, crunchy leaves are like slices of cucumber.

Last one – Wood Sorrel. Its leaves are like pale green clover, and it has these delicate white flowers. It has a sharp, tangy taste, especially in the stems, but you'd need to pick a lot of this tiny little flower to get a meal together.

Cooking with freshly foraged spring greens is a delicious joy, and a good way to get a few vitamins if you're on a wild camping mission. Am I going to make a mixed salad with some balsamic dressing? Or wilt them, and add to a creamy pasta sauce? Maybe, just sauté them in a little butter to serve as a sophisticated side dish?

Nope, I'm bunging them in with some instant noodles. They are light weight and just the type of salty junk food you're going to fancy after a long day's hike. We aren't high-brow here on the Dartmoor Podcast.

Secret ingredient - a little soy sauce, sriracha and sesame oil. Okay, that's good. Pretty damn savoury.

And I have the *evening* chorus to accompany my meal. A bit less chaotic than the dawn chorus, more laid-back, less mainstream. The hipster's choice. Time to plug in your headphones and sit tight - this is going to get really twee.

Let's see what birds are singing up on Dartmoor this evening:

This familiar little song is a Robin. Varied and musical, but thin and delicate.

And another British countryside staple, a Chaffinch. An accelerating rattle finishing with a flourish. It has been compared to the rhythm of a cricketer's run up and bowl. How unbearably English!

And that bold sound is a Song Thrush. Song Thrushes make all sorts of loud, tropical sounding cries, but you can identify them because they always repeat themselves two or three times *'lest you think he could never recapture the first fine careless rapture'*, as Robert Browning said.

We have a few migrants singing too. The Chiffchaff has flown here from Southern Europe. He basically just repeats his name, but can't even get that right, the little dunce.

He has a more elegant twin, the Willow Warbler who we can hear joining in now. Almost identical to look at, but with longer wings, as he's flown here all the way from Sub-Saharan Africa. And one big difference: that wonderful, liquid, melancholy little song. I always think it sounds like he's excited to tell you something, but then trails off embarrassedly at the end. "I saw this great documentary on traction engines the other day, it was saying that... oh, you don't care, do you?" Or, "That Malcolm from accounts is such an idiot, I can't stand the way he... he's standing behind me isn't he?"

And another long distance migrant, just arrived, and my first of the year - a Cuckoo! Dartmoor is a great place to see these very strange birds, as the open moor has so many Meadow Pipits - one of the Cuckoo's favourite hosts for their eggs.

Right, noodles eaten. Time for bed.

It's 5am on the 1st of May, and I've put the camera and microphone out to capture the ambience, then gone back to bed. If I'm not careful, one of these days, a Badger is going to run off with my GoPro.

It's a bit of a dim, drizzly morning down here in the woods, so not the perfect May the 1st! Still, you can hear that it's already pretty busy down here.

We've got a Robin and a Cuckoo, same as last night.

This pugnacious little troglodyte is a Wren - one of our smallest birds, and I always think he's trying to make up for it with his loud, rattling trill of a song.

Blue Tit. He basically just squeaks like a dog toy. Beep beep beepbeepbeep. 3 out of 10.

That sound like a broken bike pump? That's a Great Tit. 2 out of 10 if I'm being generous.

If you have good ears, you might be able to pick out a sound that is similar to the Chaffinch in rhythm – the build-up and flourish – but is incredibly high-pitched. That's a Goldcrest. Our smallest bird.

Lots of pheasants about. I heard that by mass, there is more pheasant in this country than all the other bird life put together. And Swans are pretty chunky. All so people can shoot them. Not my cup of tea, to be honest.

Our old friend the Chaffinch.

Now we have a great singer, and another warbler arrived from afar. As musical and varied as the Robin, but with a much richer timbre. The Blackcap.

The Woodpigeons have finally woken up. 'The Dartmoor Podcast, The Dartmoor Podcast', The Dartmoor Podcast's great!".

Things seem to be quietening down a little, so I'll round things up and head home. Odd that the Blackbirds have been so muted this morning. And I was hoping to capture the sound of a Pied Flycatcher or a Redstart. Let me know in the comments if I missed any!

See you next time.

EASTER EGGS, GOOFS, AND EXTRA NUGGETS

- My little brother, James, camped out with me for this one and kindly stayed out of shot and silent all through my filming just so we could do that silly Badger joke at the end. He ran the muff from my stereo microphone over the camera then carried it through the Bluebells and into a burrow. I sped it up and added the silly snuffling noises later.
- Actually, his head does appear (just!), popping up behind a log in the background at 1:23 – something I allude to in the cycling episode a few months later.
- This episode was shot near Dendles & Hawns Woods where you absolutely must not camp. Oops!

HEDGEROW ETYMOLOGY

In real life, I'm an English teacher, and, as such have a fascination in etymology - where words come from (not to be confused with entomology - beetles - although they're interesting too, I suppose.)
In this episode I look at some edible Dartmoor plants and, these often have some quite unusual names. Here's where they come from!

Hogweed

My favourite edible plant. You'd suspect that the name is because pigs like to eat them, but there is some evidence that the real reason is that the plant smells a bit like pigs. Now, I haven't sniffed a pig recently, so I can't confirm this. Its other name is Cow Parsnip, with the 'pars' bit being an old French reference to using a pronged fork digging up the ground, and the 'nip' being derived from 'neep' an old name for a Turnip.

Jack-by-the-hedge

A proper folksy old name that one! The 'by the hedge' bit is pretty straightforward, but the 'Jack' bit is more of a puzzle. One theory is that 'Jack' is an old euphemistic name for the devil, whose breath, supposedly, smells of garlic. Very suitable for this plant whose other name is 'Garlic Mustard'. 'Garlic', by the way, has a pretty interesting etymology too –'Gar' meaning spear, referring to those pointy leaves, and 'lic' coming from 'Leek'. A spear leek!

Dandelion

The folky name of 'Piss-a-bed' is pretty self-explanatory, but the more common name from this plant comes from French - 'Dent-de-lion', meaning 'teeth of the lion' to describe the jagged leaves.

Wood Sorrell

Another tasty little plant I pick in this episode. The 'Wood' part is, again a pretty obvious reference to where the plant grows, but the 'Sorrel' is more interesting, deriving from the word 'sour'. Very apt, as it has a slightly tangy, zesty flavour. Another name for this plant is 'Cuckoo Sorrel' which I assumed was linked to the time of year it could be found... but no! There is an old myth where the Cuckoo has to eat this plant before it can sing.

Herb Robert

'Herb' is another one of those old words that refer to all sorts of plants, but the 'Robert' bit here is more of a mystery. It's possibly linked to 'Robin Goodfellow', another name for 'Puck'... A 'Pucksie'... A Pixie! Very apt for Dartmoor. It is perhaps this association with the supernatural tricksters that another name for this plant is 'Death-come-quickly' due to the superstition that if you pick this plant and take it home, a death will soon follow. Oddly, and in contrast to this, it was widely considered a miracle cure for all sorts of things. This plant has a ridiculous number of other folk names that I don't have space to explain here: Red Robin, Storksbill, Stinking Bob, Kiss-me-love-at-the-garden-gate, Squinter Pip, Jack Horner, Crow's Foot, Witch's Foot, Bloodwort,

Dragon's Blood, Dolly's Nightcap, Dolly's Pinafore, Dolly's Apron, Doly's Shoes, Felonwort, and Fox Geranium. Blimey!

THE DARTMOOR PODCAST EPISODE FOUR

04/06/2022

SEARCH FOR PIXIES HOUSE

DIGNIFIED

EPISODE REVIEW

Now we're talking! This feels like a proper Dartmoor Podcast* episode. It looks really good (I think this must have been where I worked out how to stabilise the video and tinker with the colour and contrast), and it has a good mix of silliness and thoughtfulness.

I have very fond memories of filming this one, too. It was a real adventure, and one of the most beautiful days out I can recall – the serene churchyard in the village, the views of Burrator Reservoir from on top of Sheepstor, the Dartmoor Ponies among the Bluebells, and the clear and starry night. Ah!

Also, this is the first episode where I feel like I learnt something. The information on Woodpeckers, birdsong, and forageable munchies in the previous episodes was just me passing on some of my factoids, but this required research. One of the greatest gifts the Dartmoor Podcast* has given me is that it's pushed me to keep expanding my knowledge on all sorts of subjects.

There are plenty of people out there who really do believe in Pixies, and I think this is why this video got me my first ever 'dislike'!

SCRIPT

You won't find a square mile of Dartmoor that doesn't have some sort of mythical beastie roaming it. We've got ghosts, witches, devils, panthers, murderous disembodied hands, and we're practically tripping over spectral hounds.

But today, I'm going to be investigating Dartmoor's most famous cryptozoological creatures - the pixies, or, as they are called in the true, old Westcountry dialect, 'the piskies'!

This should be a really fun one. The mission: to trek up to the impressive granite mass of Sheepstor and search for a hidden cave marked on the OS map as 'Pixies House'. A place, known for centuries as a haunt of the little folk, and where people would go to leave them gifts and gain their favour.

I should warn you, that the journey we are embarking on is a mysterious and bewildering nightmare of conflicting information. A soup of rumours, misconstrued facts, barefaced lies and unsubstantiated claims. It's enough to make you want to bang your head against the Meavy Oak!

Welcome back to the Dartmoor Podcast!

What's a pixie? As a birder and all-round nature geek, I like to taxonomize things - I like to know how to identify something, put a name to it, note its salient features, and explain its behaviours. And this just isn't going to happen with the pixies - some stories have them invisibly small, some sitting under toadstools, some the size of children, and some even larger. Some stories describe them as being naked, some wearing rags, and others dressing them in the floppy hats and green cloaks. Do they have wings or not? Again, accounts are conflicted.

And there's an infuriating inconsistency in their behaviour, too! What do Pixies do? Well, whatever they like, apparently! The legends don't paint them as 'evil' beings, nor benevolent ones - rather, mischievous agents of chaos. On a whim, they might lead you off the path and leave you lost amongst the mires of the moors, or they might help you with your housework. They might take you on a magical moonlight dance across their fairy kingdom, or they might just steal your child and replace them with one of their own.

Oh, dear I said the 'F' word. Fairies. Are Pixies fairies? On the face of it, it seems pretty obvious that they are. But in the go-to Pixie text, 'A Peep at the Pixies' (a Victorian collection of stories about them), the author, Mrs Bray claims that they are distinct races, and that the Pixies actually fought and won a war against the Fairies on the Somerset border to keep them out of Devon.

But Mrs Anna Eliza Bray is the first of this episode's fibbers. 'A Peep at the Pixies' is a fun read, but Mrs Bray has a habit of espousing rather wild and fanciful theories as facts, especially when discussing the druids. If her book were a Wikipedia article, it would be littered with 'citation neededs'.

Anyway, I'm determined not to take Mrs Bray as an authority on anything pixie-related. It seems she travelled down to the Westcountry to collect stories of the fair folk, and was no doubt strung along with a few tall tales from the locals, especially as she seemed to view them with some contempt. Allow me, briefly, to besmirch your opinion of her further by reading an excerpt from the introduction to her book where she describes the inhabitants of Dartmoor:

"The people who live in these humble dwellings are not very nice, for the pig-stye is generally near the door, and the children are not much cleaner than the pigs. It is the more discreditable to their mothers to let them be so, as there is water enough around to wash and keep clean all the children in Devonshire."

How dare she!

Anyhow, I suppose there's a simple reason that the appearance and behaviour of Pixies is somewhat fluid - they don't exist.

But that doesn't make them any less interesting!

One thing that certainly does exist is 'Pixies House', a naturally formed cave on the south side of Sheepstor, hidden among the granite clitter. This should prove easier to find than the Lustleigh Nutcracker of episode one, because I was actually able to find some good descriptions of where it's located. Whether or not it would be easy to get to, or get *in* to, however, would be another matter entirely.

Briefly, on the topic of a 'Pixie House', an interesting little fact that popped up in my research, is that the earliest recorded version of the world renowned *Three Little Pigs* story comes from Dartmoor, and rather than pigs and a wolf, stars Pixies whose houses are blown down by a fox.

My walk began at Yelverton, and took me through the beautiful little village of Meavy, which seems to be built around an impressive Oak tree - the Meavy Oak, estimated to be over a thousand years old. It is said that King Charles hid up this particular tree when running from Cromwell's men in the English civil war.

And that isn't even the only fleeing from Cromwell story of the day! I next visited Burrator Reservoir, to see the remains of Longstone Manor. You see, Longstone Manor was the home of John Elford back in the 15th century, an artist and a nobleman who ended up on the wrong side of Cromwell. But rather than sequestering himself up a tree, Elford had a much more cunning hiding place - Pixies House, explaining its other name 'Elford's Cave'. Apparently he passed his time in hiding by painting on the granite walls, though no evidence of this remains.

In fact, Elford's name seems to pop up all over the place on this part of the moor. On my way up to the cave, I couldn't resist popping in to Sheepstor Village - a tiny hamlet with a beautiful graveyard, where an example of John Elford's artwork is displayed above the door of the church. A skull, on an hourglass, with corn growing through the eye sockets. Bit creepy, that, mate!

And then finally to Sheepstor itself. I wonder why they call it that?

Now, to find the cave itself I managed to print off a couple of photos which show the right angle of approach, and one which highlights that the cave is situated between a small oak and a holly growing amongst the boulders of the tor. And once I've scrambled up there, I'm looking for this little crevice.

This wasn't as easy as I thought it would be. For starters, there is no hidden little trail as there often is to such places, I really had to find my own way there using the small trees as guides, and it involved some quite tricky scrambling and rock-hopping across wobbly boulders. It would certainly make an excellent hideout for an outlaw nobleman. I'd have had no chance of finding it without the detailed photos and descriptions from the internet.

And then there was the cave itself. Genuinely quite unwelcoming. I have to admit that I considered wimping out here. The thought of getting trapped in that hidden little hole with no one around to call out to for help. Oh, and the potential embarrassment of it being caught on camera, too! Despite it being a nice day, the wind seemed to blow a little colder, and the crows wheeled overhead suspiciously, the braying of the sheep became a mocking cry, and some dogs barked threateningly in the distance.

No. I wasn't coming all the way out here for nothing.

I had to literally slither on my belly to squeeze through the gap, and managed to bump my head and my knee on the way in. And once in, it was much smaller and danker than I expected, hardly room to stand, though perhaps room to lay out a small bed if you were desperate to stay concealed.

And there were far fewer gifts for the pixies than I expected, too! A creepy little doll, a few old scraps of ribbon, a glass bead, and a few coins tossed onto a ledge. It seems that the Pixies really have been largely forgotten.

The coolest thing in the cave, though, was this patch of bioluminescent fungus, glowing eerily from the inner wall of a deeper little chamber.

The obvious, twee, podcasty thing to do here would have been to leave my own gift, to bring me luck and protection from the pixies. Especially as I was planning on wild camping out in unfamiliar territory that evening. But then I thought, what if I don't? Let's put my rational disbelief in the fair folk to the test. Yes, I decided to deliberately antagonise the pixies in the hope that they'd give me a visit and shake me to my empirical core.

And, I thought I'd take this one step further, by camping under a Hawthorn tree. You see, Hawthorns, particularly lone Hawthorns, have long been associated with the supernatural as portals to the fairy realm. It is also known as the Whitethorn or May Tree, as, at this time of year, it blooms in a frothing mass of pure white flowers. There have been several of them hidden in this video already.

The hawthorn in May is an impressive tree, standing out like a white beacon amongst the greens and browns of the moor. The bark is hard and gnarled, with the branches thrusting forth rows of sharp needles. Up close it hums and fizzes with pollinating insects. And then there's the smell. Unlike the sweet, floral scent of other flowers, the Hawthorn carries the rotten stench of death, decay, and bodily fluids. And perhaps this surprising, unnatural odour accounts for its links with the mystical.

Surely, after dissing the Pixies in their own house, then sleeping at the entrance of a pixie-portal, they would visit me in the night and give me a fright. They are famous for administering a pretty severe pinching to those who offend them - something I am willing to risk if it proves the existence of a supernatural race of forgotten little people.

Assuming then, perhaps prematurely, that Pixies don't exist, the most interesting question is then *why* did people believe in them?

One theory is that they are a corrupted memory of an pre-historic race. A common element of the Fairy myth, wherever it is told, is that they are afraid of iron, and you could imagine that when the Celts made their Iron Age foray onto this island, they may have encountered isolated Stone Age tribes who were easily defeated by superior metal weapons. Perhaps these people were short of stature, and perhaps they scattered to hide in the forests and hills of ancient Britain to play spiteful tricks on those of their conquerors who became lost in the woods. Eventually encounters with these people would become a rarity, then a rumour, then a myth.

Or perhaps, Fairies are just a way to explain away the inexplicable. In a pre-science society, when your crops failed, or someone was struck with a sudden illness, or a child went missing, the simplest explanation would be to personify the cause. It was the little folk. This is particularly sinister, when considering the 'changeling' myth associated with the Fairies. If a child grew up to have what we might now understand as a developmental condition, the parents may have preferred to believe that their 'real' child had been taken to the Fairy Kingdom and replaced with a Pixie.

You'd think that the arrival of Christianity might have quelled some of these superstitions, and to an extent it did. But some clergymen saw an opportunity to use the myth to their advantage, saying that Pixies *did* exist, and that they were the souls of unbaptised children, no less.

Then despite the great scientific and technological advances made in the Victorian and Edwardian eras, there actually seems to have been an increase in Fairy belief. Think of Willam Blake observing a 'fairy funeral', or our Mrs Bray, or even the fake photo case of the Cottingley Fairies. This could be precisely *because* of these great leaps forward. It was a push back against rationalism. When the scalpel of science was peeling away the mysteries of the world people, sad at its loss, had a *desire* to believe in the magical.

And there's one more theory to explain the origins of the Fairy myth. One that not many people talk about. Putting all superstition and speculation aside, perhaps it's time to admit that Pixies are, that's right, you guessed it... *aliens*.

Little people with strange powers, flight, crop circles and fairy rings, animal mutilations, people being abducted then returned with a sense of lost time. There are more than a few similarities between these two camps. As Arthur C Clarke famously said, *"Any sufficiently advanced technology is indistinguishable from magic"* - were the people of the past meeting extra-terrestrials, but so unable to conceive of their technology that they perceived them, instead, as enchanted beings?

Probably not.

As dusk settled on the land like a blanket of soot, I drowsed into dark dreams under the decaying blooms of the Whitethorn. Dreams of alien craft arcing through inky skies, giddy waltzes across the black moor, a changeling crowning from a rocky womb, twisted trees raising kings in their stunted branches, skulls grinning from the sands of time. Then woke up pinched black and blue by the Pixies.

Not really. Despite me antagonising the Pixies into showing themselves, I didn't hear a peep out of them.

And after me criticising Mrs Bray for her lack of verified sources in her work, I think it's only fair if I give you a run-down of some other things in this episode which probably aren't true -

King Charles probably didn't hide up the Meavy Oak. Many other trees hold similar claims.

John Elford probably didn't hide in 'Elford's Cave'. This started as a rumour because someone paintings were found on the walls of the cave in the 17th Century.

Sheepstor isn't named after sheep. It seems to have evolved through many names over the years: Sitelestorra, Skytelestor, Shittestorre, Shistor, Shetelstor, Shepstor.

Not all species of Hawthorn smell bad.

All the pixie origin stories are highly speculative.

Who would have thought that the 'Three Little Pigs' bit was true!

So, the 'Piskies House' turned out to be a neglected and forgotten little chamber hidden away on this beautiful part of the moor. It feels like the world has moved on from the Pixies - something which my Dartmoor hero, the Reverend Sabine Baring Gould, saw all the way back in the 1800s. I will leave you with his wise words:

Superstition is dead now on Dartmoor, as elsewhere, and ghosts as well as pixies have been banished, not as the old moormen say, by the "ding-dongs" of the church and mission chapel bells, but by the voice of the schoolmaster.

Thanks for listening.

EASTER EGGS, GOOFS, AND EXTRA NUGGETS

- Starting by hoiking the camera out of a hole is a nice reference to the end of the previous episode, that I imagine most viewers will have completely missed. I like the idea that all Badger burrows on Dartmoor are somehow magically connected.
- I really do bang my head against that metal pole on the Meavey Oak, and that is the real sound of my few remaining braincells dying. I also banged my head pretty hard on the roof of Pixies House. Maybe that's why this episode is so dreamy.
- There's a cheeky little *Close Encounters of the Third Kind* reference in the night-lapse scene played with harmonics on my guitar.
- The music at the end over the fact corrections is a twee acoustic cover of *Where is my Mind* by… The Pixies!

STAY ON THE GOOD SIDE OF THE PISKIES

A number of interesting superstitions have arisen around the Pixies on Dartmoor, and although the little blighters don't exist, that doesn't stop them being a complete menace. Here are some tips to stay out of Pixie trouble.

Pixie Prevention:

A few items are said to help keep the fair folk away. They hate iron, so carry a pin or other small item made of this metal. Items associated with Christianity are also said to protect you – holy water, bells, bread, and crosses. A cross made out of Rowan wood is supposedly especially effective.

Pixie-led:

If you forgot to pack any of the above items and find yourself inexplicably lost on Dartmoor, you are probably being 'pixie-led' and will stumble around 'mazed' for hours unless you do something to escape.

The most common solution is to turn an item of clothing inside-out, which supposedly throws the pixies off your trail. Against all my rational senses, after being well and truly lost, I have actually resorted to turning a glove inside out, and I almost immediately realised where I'd gone wrong.

Make of that what you will.

I've also heard that smearing yourself in cow pats or other animal dung will work, as the Pixies hate dirt. I have not resorted to this. Yet.

Pixie Avoidance:

According to Pixie experts (experts on Pixies, not highly-qualified Fairies), there are a few things to absolutely avoid if you want to stay out of trouble. Definitely don't step into a fairy ring, keep away from lone Hawthorns, and avoid picking Stitchwort.

General Good Practice:

On the whole, you should try and be polite and courteous to the Pixies, even leaving them little treats or trinkets if you want their favour. Try not to antagonise them by saying they don't exist or calling them names like 'Stinkerbell', 'Short Arse' or 'Gnome Features' .

THE DARTMOOR PODCAST EPISODE FIVE

11/08/2022

SEARCH FOR SHERBERTON STREAM

SPLASHING ABOUT LIKE A DAFT OLD HIPPIE

EPISODE REVIEW

And another! These aren't bad are they? I'd probably not rush this as much nowadays as I've grown more confident in my 'craft', but I also like that it doesn't drag on, I suppose.

While filming at Buckfast Abbey and trying to find the Salmon steps a seagull crapped all over me… I mean, absolutely everywhere - a really bad one. I ended up, at about six in the morning, hunched over a little water-feature in the abbey grounds trying to wash seagull poop out of my hair. Then a monk strolled past and gave me a look of absolute horror - his serene morning meditation ruined by some shit-covered goblin man splashing about in his fountain.

I wish I had got some more of the underwater footage, but it was actually really busy by the 'secret' Sherberton Stream when I found it. By the time the families had packed up and left, the sun had gone in and it was properly freezing!

Nice to see some literature creeping in to this episode - it was only a matter of time! Oswald's *Dart* and Deakin's *Waterlog* both go on my list of recommendations.

SCRIPT

[extract from *Dart* not included here for copyright reasons]

That was from *Dart* by the poet Alice Oswald. A 48 page poem describing the River Dart's sinuous journey from source to mouth. The River Dart, the very river that gives my favourite place its name.

Welcome back to the Dartmoor Podcast!

Now, Oswald's poem is based on conversations with real people met along the Dart. And one of the people mentioned, is a wonderful eccentric environmentalist called Roger Deakin. And it turns out that I had his book at home. It's a book on wild swimming. *The* book on wild swimming, in fact. *Waterlog* [Look signed copy!]. It documents Deakin's adventures as he attempts to swim all over the British isles.

The whole book's a beautiful read - full of personality - written with all with the charm, poetry and humour of that particular type of daft old hippie you'd expect to find splashing around in a hidden pool.

Deakin's passion for wild swimming is completely infectious. And, of course, he swims in the Dart.

And when I was wading through the wonderful whimsy of *Waterlog*, this caught my imagination.

[extract from *Waterlog* not included here for copyright reasons]

I couldn't let that go, could I?

Sherberton stream! A secret location teeming with giant salmon! Could I find this place? And if I could, would the Salmon still congregate there 20 years later? It would certainly be an adventure to find out.

Now, as absurdly niche as it might seem, I'm not the first person to try this. A quick google led me to a blog by a chap called Joe Minihane called 'Waterlog Reswum' where he recounts swimming in the River Dart near the village of Sherberton on Dartmoor... except I am pretty sure he was in the wrong place. For starters, Our wily merman Roger Deakin surely wouldn't make it that easy to find his hidden stream, and I believe that the popular swimming spot described in the blog was a red herring [no fish pun intended... but then I didn't leave it out, either]. It just doesn't add up - Joe's spot lacks the steep oak and holly sided valley, and, furthermore, Joe, with a charmingly self-deprecating manner, thinks he was in the wrong place, too.

Most importantly, though, as I was reading Deakin's description of the salmon pool, a little light went on in my head: I *think* I might actually know where this is! A quick look at the map revealed a subtle connection with the name Sherberton which cemented the possibility in my mind. I'm not going to tell you where it is by the way - far be it for me to ruin the decades old secret of the late Roger Deacon and his friend! I suppose a few keen-eyed Dartmoor afficionados might be able to work it out from my video, but then I'm capable of throwing in a little deception too!

Next, I took a long tumble down the Google rabbit-hole and became fascinated by the crazy life-cycle of the Dartmoor Salmon. I have a new-found respect for the fish, and after this very simplified explanation, I hope you'll like Salmon, too [oh dear].

The baby Salmon hatch from thousands of eggs high up in the shallow gravelly stretches of the Dart. There they slowly grow to maturity over about four years, then undergo a massive physiological change to become capable of surviving in salt water, before rushing out to sea to live out their adult life.

There, North Atlantic Salmon may travel many thousands of miles and grow into voracious predators as they hunt smaller fish in the seas around Iceland and Greenland. They may live out there in the dark and icy seas for anywhere up to four years, and the longer they do, the larger they grow.

Then one day, they get the sudden urge to return home.

This is the truly extraordinary part. These fish somehow find their way back to the same river they were born in, overcoming incredible obstacles on the way. Dodging predators, fighting the currents, and leaping up weirs and waterfalls. Even more insane, they do all of this without eating. You see, once the Salmon re-enters their birthing river, they cease to feed. It's as if they knows that this is their last journey - their final purpose. After spawning, they weaken and die.

If Deakin's giant Salmon are still to be found in Sherberton Stream, then they will be grizzled veterans of the open ocean returning to their home river for the last time. They will be waiting patiently and fasting through the summer months in the cold, dark, oxygen rich waters waiting for a late summer storm to flood the river and allow them to swim the last few miles to their breeding grounds.

You won't be surprised to learn that, along with almost all the nature in this country, Salmon numbers are declining. In the 80s, an average of 330 fish a year were caught on the Dart - in 2019, just 14.

So I was glad to hear that a few things are being done. For starters, a byelaw states that all Salmon caught on the Dart before 16th June must be put back, and it is strongly encouraged that they are released all-year round.

And secondly, just last year, here at the majestic Buckfast Abbey, a set of Salmon Steps were built to help the creatures navigate a tricky weir on their return to their spawning grounds. I couldn't seem to get to it though.

In fact everything on this journey was more difficult than it first appeared! If Sherberton Stream, as Deakin claimed, joined the Dart on the left as you swam down the river, then I would simply need to cross the Dart and walk up the opposite bank until I hit it. Easier said than done! From the direction I approached, the path was very overgrown, and in places it had slipped away and fallen into the Dart. Progress was slow, and I began to worry that I'd overshot, and that Sherberton Stream had simply dried up in July's drought.

But then I found it, just as Deakin had described - a very cold stream trickling down the valley side under the shade of Oaks and Hollies. Perfect.

You could actually feel the difference in temperature here above and below where the stream met the Dart.

Would the cold, oxygenated water attract the big fish?

The water was a little cloudier than I'd hoped, and it was so cold, I only went for relatively quick dip, but as you can see, there were fish in there! Some of them were definitely Salmon, and I saw one quite large fish – maybe a foot long. This is the biggest one I caught on camera, but I think he's a trout due to the spots covering his entire body.

Anyway, a moderate success! I found the secret Sherberton Stream and found some reasonably large fish. One quick dip doesn't really prove that Salmon have declined here, and maybe on another day, I'd have had a similar experience to Deakin. It was a wonderful spot for a swim, so I'll definitely be back.

Anyway, there was one last thing Deakin mentioned that I'd like to give a go.

Thanks for watching!

EASTER EGGS, GOOFS, AND EXTRA NUGGETS

- I suppose you'd like to know where Sherberton Stream is wouldn't you? Ah – go on then! It's actually very simple. A little way up from the popular swimming spot of Sharrah Pool is Meltor Wood, and running through these woods is a stream called Simons Lake that starts as a spring on… Sherberton Common! Simons Lake is the real Sherberton Stream, and where it meets the Dart is the legendary Salmon pool.
- The Dartmoor Podcast* font (Sunday) is finally here! Sadly it looks really grainy due to my editing incompetence.
- I cut out a particularly silly joke from this episode where I said 'I hope you like Salmon too' vaguely to the rhythm of Bob Marley's 'I hope you like jammin' too'. I regret this immensely and wish I'd left it in. Nothing ever got left out again no matter how ridiculous.
- A silly little joke that did survive is when I'm researching on the laptop - I type in 'Do Salmon bite people?'
- Talk Talk *Spirt of Eden* is possibly the most under-appreciated album ever and I have no qualms about advertising it here on my swimming t-shirt.

SALMON LIFE CYCLE

I practically skipped over this amazing natural phenomenon in the episode as I couldn't be bothered looking into all the silly little names the Salmon gets as it goes through its various life stages. In hindsight, it's actually quite interesting, so here you go!

Pea-sized **eggs** laid in gravel streams.

Alevins – freaky little newly hatched Salmon with yolks still attached.

Fry (as in 'small fry').

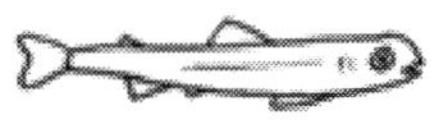

Parr – develop blotchy camouflage that I forgot to draw, and don't intend to now. They live in the river in this state for one to three years before smolting...

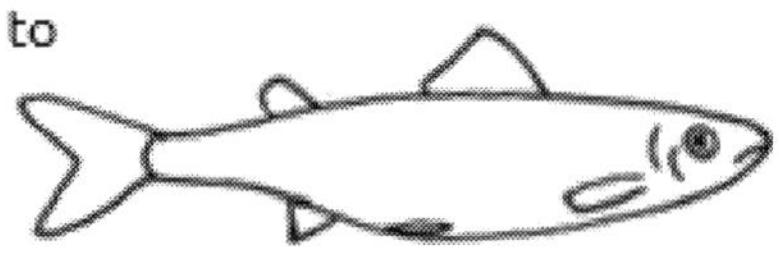

Smolt – the Salmon undergo all sorts of physical changes that prepare them for life in salt-water then head out to sea. This one looks particularly stressed about the whole thing.

Grilse – adult Salmon mostly spend a year at sea then return to their home rivers... but some stay out there for up to three years and become whoppers.

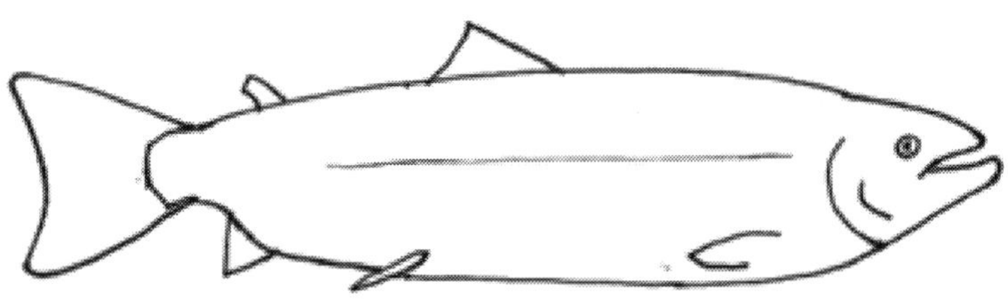

THE DARTMOOR PODCAST EPISODE SIX

11/09/2022

SEARCH FOR THE CRANMERE POOL LETTERBOX

FIRST GUESTS!

EPISODE REVIEW

My first foray into getting guests on! I don't think many people are lucky enough to find great friends in their place of work, but I have been blessed in this respect. Dave and Tom are teachers of History and Geography respectively, and both bloody great blokes. Dave gets to be star of this episode because of his sad geocaching obsession. Tom will be back in the future!

I wish I'd sat down and interviewed Dave rather than just getting him on audio, but I hadn't quite worked out how to do that yet.

On the rewatch, I love the contrast between the weather of the East and North Moor!

SCRIPT

In 1854, a Dartmoor walking guide from Chagford called James Perrot, walked out onto the north moor, and left a bottle in the middle of nowhere. The idea was that you could trek out there, find the bottle, and leave a stamped postcard addressed to yourself, which the next finder would then post back to you.

This is typical of those Victorians, who, suddenly finding themselves with a lot of time on their hands and the means to travel about, invented all sorts of daft sports and pastimes to keep themselves entertained. [see football, tennis, rugby, cycling etc.]

Over the next century, 'letterboxing' evolved into a full-blown hobby, with many more 'letterboxes' being hidden on the moor.

Exciting stuff – a whole world of secret, hidden messages hidden under the granite boulders we wander past while out for a moorland walk.

As a man renowned for his whimsy, who loves riddles, mysteries and puzzles, and for whom Dartmoor is a second home, it seems crazy that I hadn't got into this before.

I dug into an old book of my grandparents' by Anne Swincombe [Anne Swincow] to find out a little more about how Letterboxing had evolved since the Victorian era.

Nowadays, there are thousands of these secret containers out there, and once you locate one and look inside, you'll find a notebook and a stamp, so you can prove you found it.

Once you have proof of 100 boxes found, you can send off for a special '100 club' badge. Surely an ambition for a future episode!

But for now, I just wanted to get started. Little did I know that I was going to be put through a whole range of challenges, and was to experience one of the strangest things that have ever happened to me on the moors!

Welcome back to the Dartmoor Podcast.

(cough) I said the Dartmoor Podcast [not a Podcast]. That's better! [I have committed to this joke]

On a scorching August day, I headed up to the eastern fringe of the moor, to look for my first letterboxes. I armed myself with a map, compass, ink pad, personalised stamp, and most importantly, the 'Spring 2022 catalogue of Dartmoor Letterboxes'. The book is updated twice yearly to account for any new boxes added and to remove any boxes which have vanished.

You look up the map square you are visiting in the index to find the names of letterboxes hidden in that area, and then find the alphabetically listed details for each specific box. This usually includes a more accurate 6-figure grid reference, and some landmarks that can be seen from the box with compass coordinates so that you can triangulate its position. There may be some other clues or riddles, too.

I, rather ambitiously, listed the names of eight or nine boxes in the Bowerman's nose area, and naively set off ready to harvest those inky stamps of goodness. Here are some lessons I learnt very quickly:

Firstly, it is difficult. Really tricky. They seem to be very well hidden, and the compass bearings are hard to use to pinpoint the boxes, as they might include something like 'the Rowan Tree', when there are several visible!

Secondly, don't go Letterboxing in the height of summer. The hard-to-find boxes are even harder to find when there is shoulder-high bracken everywhere. Also, you could end up disturbing breeding birds which no one wants. Oh, and its hot. And there are ticks. I'm definitely saving any push for my 100 club badge until it gets a bit cooler.

And thirdly, bring your own ink pad. Some boxes seem to include an ink pad for your stamp, but not all. And even if a pad is in place, it might have dried up or got soggy and watered-down.

Anyway, without giving away any locations, I did find a couple, and got the satisfaction of whacking my first stamps in my notebook. But there were many more I didn't find. Here's a timelapse of me miserably failing to find any letterboxes.

Eventually, I retreated to the shade of some rocks for a cup of tea, to reflect on my progress so far. But even this relaxing break was cut short by an absolutely extraordinary quantity of ticks, no doubt due to the local sheep also taking advantage of the shady spots around the tor. My usual system for dealing with ticks is to wear these very pale-faded grey jeans so that I can catch the little buggers crawling up, then flick them into oblivion, but these were so numerous and tiny that a few were getting past my defences.

On my way back to the shady woods for a refreshing dip in the Bovey, it occurred to me that the one thing that would certainly assist in finding more boxes would be more pairs of eyes.

Luckily, I knew just the people.

My mates Dave and Tom are always up for a ramble on the moor, and Dave, in particular, is a keen geocacher.

And I had just the mission to tempt them out - A pilgrimage to that first ever letterbox left by James Perrot in 1854. What is now known as 'The Cranmere Pool Letterbox'.

One small snag though – I was going to have to leave my comfortable, sunny, friendly Hobbiton part of the moor and head up to Mordor [Okehampton].

Still, at least the weather said it would be a nice day.

Undeterred, we set off on the long walk towards out prize. And Dave had even highlighted a number of geocaches we could find on the way. Here's Dave on the subject!

(Geocaches are essential a modern evolution of the letterbox, being a hidden cache that you can find with the help of GPS coordinates on your phone. And rather than just being on Dartmoor, geocaches have spread all over the world.)

Dave on geocaching.

With the extra eyes, and Dave's expertise, we were finding geocaches left, right and centre while all the time drawing closer to our main prize.

Dave on geocaching and letterboxing.

With plenty of miles to walk over this imposing and impressive landscape, we had plenty of time to reflect on why people were drawn to these niche activities.

Dave on why.

The plan was to keep using the old military roads to get as close as possible to our destination, before heading off road to follow the West Okement river that would lead us to the boggy depression known as Cranmere Pool. The letterbox is actually on the OS maps, so I don't think I'm breaking any letterboxing code by revealing the location here!

Dave talking about secrecy.

Eventually, we reached a small pond, rather mysteriously named Ockerton Court, where the road ended. This area of Dartmoor was particularly featureless and bleak, and we were going to have to head off the trail.

Dave on favourite Caches.

Well, we were certainly heading somewhere remote. The path got smaller, and smaller, and smaller until there was no path at all. The combination of damp, tall grass, an uneven surface, and no way of seeing over the next ridge made this deeply, deeply unpleasant. I had assumed that although Cranmere Pool was a remote and 'secret' location there would be a little path or 'desire line', if you will, leading to the letterbox. If there was, we didn't find it.

But after about half an hour of stumbling around in the mizzle, we arrived, right on top of it!

No mere bottle in a bank, over the years, the letterbox has been upgraded several times, and now boasts a solid concrete shell and a sturdy metal door.

And once inside, we were in Letterbox heaven. A proper logbook signed by hundreds of likeminded travellers, and, of course, the all-precious stamp of the place that started it all.

Such a strange thing to find in such a bleak and desolate place! No wonder Cranmere pool has developed a number of spooky myths and legends… but perhaps we'll save them for another day.

We signed the book, adding our name to the list of letterboxers that stretches back over a hundred years, and made ourselves a tiny part of that history.

After our slog into the pool, there was no question of returning the same way, and we started to follow what seemed to be a path back towards the north, but again, this path soon disappeared and left us stumbling around the deeply vegetated boggy ground. And I realised that I'd lost my map. Despite a quick, frantic search where we attempted to retrace our steps, it was gone, lost somewhere in the waving green sea of Molinia.

No matter, with the help of Dave's GPS we eventually bundled back onto the military roads at Ockerton Court, and I felt sure I knew my way around from there, so was confident to say goodbye to Dave and Tom while I went in search of a place to camp out.

But, alone now, as I climbed higher towards the peaks of Yes Tor and the High Wilhays, the clouds came in with renewed force and slicing winds. My earlier confidence in where I was began to evaporate, and I really wished I had my map, when… I found a map. Not my map, but a different map. Just lying on the ground, right in my path. I was grateful for exactly what I needed, but it was a coincidence to set my mind reeling!

Anyway, finally, to the exciting bit. You see, this whole adventure has led me to decide to set up a letterbox of my own! You should soon be able to find this by ordering the next Dartmoor Letterbox Catalogue, but in the meantime I'll give you a clue.

Ahem.

Wanderer above a sea of fog,
Searched for a rock that wouldn't log.
Between a Raven and a Chest,
Lies a Pixie's writing desk.
Once this location you have found,
My letterbox is nigh around.

And I shall be adding a Dartmoor Podcast geocache in the vicinity, too, if that is more your thing!

As an added clue, I should say that watching my first ever video – the Search for the Nutcracker, will help with the clues.

I have a suspicion that this won't be the last time we discuss letterboxes on this channel, and I can only imagine what adventures this new angle on Dartmoor exploration might lead me to. Thanks very much for listening to another ramble.

See you next time!

EASTER EGGS, GOOFS, AND EXTRA NUGGETS

- The sunny scenes on East Dartmoor are actually filmed *after* the North Moor stuff. It's all lies!
- ...Except for the weird incident of losing and finding the map – that's not staged. You can genuinely see how amazed I am just from the back of my head.
- The Dartmoor Podcast* geocache is at N50°37'11.118 W3°44'13.38. Or if you prefer a 'What Three Words' it's shield.extra.discusses.

FIND THE DARTMOOR PODCAST* LETTERBOX!

At the time of writing *no-one* has found the Dartmoor Podcast* letterbox (and at the time of editing, it's only been found once - by letterboxing legends Rat Boy and Si of Relief)! I sometimes worry that I put it in quite an 'un-letterboxy' place and am somehow going against the guidelines.

It's a shame as there's a nice stamp in there, just waiting to be used, though you would need to bring your own ink.

I'll deconstruct the riddle for you so you someone can finally find it!

WANDERER ABOVE THE SEA OF FOG
SEARCHED FOR A ROCK THAT WOULDN'T LOG

(it's near where that 'wanderer pose' was taken in episode one about the 'logging' rock)

BETWEEN A RAVEN AND A CHEST,
LIES A PIXIE'S WRITING DESK

(The spot is located between Ravens Tor and Harton Chest. The 'pixie's writing desk' is an interesting thing! There's a little chair and desk from a dolls' house positioned in a little rock cave there – it's been there for over a decade now.)

ONCE THIS LOCATION YOU HAVE FOUND,
MY LETTERBOX IS NIGH AROUND.

(It isn't in the same pile of rocks as the dolls' furniture, but under a nearby rock a little up the slope.)

The full bearings and coordinates are as follows: Bowerman's Nose 241, Left side of Houndtor 218, Trendlebere Carpark 163, Pixie's Desk 338, and 30 paces NW.

THE DARTMOOR PODCAST EPISODE SEVEN

21/09/2022

CYCLING THE DARTMOOR WAY

PHOTOBOMBED BY A VICAR

EPISODE REVIEW

This is a nice episode, isn't it? Nice vibes. Just a pair of brothers going on an adventure together. Honestly, I'd like a bit more of a surprising tangent or lateral twist for my ideal Dartmoor Podcast* episode, but this is a very calming watch.

James's one, barely audible, contribution to the episode is to call me a 'sefie-stick wanker', which tells you all you need to know about our relationship. Seriously, though, he did a lot of work in planning and organising the whole thing, so well done my beardy brother.

I'd completely forgotten about the 'Nathan' incident and feel a bit bad about how flippant I am about it here. The poor animal absolutely legged it and the girl leading him was genuinely distressed as she charged after him along the road shouting 'Nathan! Nathan! Nathan!' (possibly). Some people say she's still chasing Nathan across the moor to this day... And now I'm being flippant again.

SCRIPT

Here on the Dartmoor Podcast [not a podcast], my missions tend to be about finding some obscure geographical feature or animal, but this time round I'm attempting something a little different – an adventure that is more about the journey than the destination, so to speak.

Earlier this year, The Dartmoor Way was officially opened – a route for walkers or cyclists that circumnavigates Dartmoor in its entirety, linking all the little towns, villages and hamlets that cling to its fringes.

Would a man who had been surviving on a diet of craft beer and crisps, with a severely knackered mountain bike, and none of the correct equipment, be able to cycle all the way around Dartmoor in two days?

Maybe with some help. Luckily, my brother, James, was also up for the challenge and knew a thing or two about bikes and cycling. He has been a guest on the Podcast [not a podcast] before, in episode 3, as I'm sure you remember.

James plotted the route using his fancy cycling computer and strava and whatnot, but here's me drawing a line on a map to pretend I had something to do with it and create a pleasing visual device to explain the route.

We would start at Tavistock, cycle anti-clockwise around the south of the moor via Ivybridge, then spend the night in Bovey Tracey before heading north and arcing past Mordor [Okehampton] on the way back to the start.

The route, in total, would be 143 kilometres (about 89 miles in old money), and perhaps more worryingly, included 2,493 metres (8,179 feet) of elevation, meaning a lot of slogging up hills.

If you've seen any of my wild camping kit reviews, you'll know that I don't look after anything. My bike needed a new tyre and the brakes changing as well as some work doing on the gears. This is my favourite bit [a broken man]!

Early on the morning of August the 27th, we headed off on a beautiful drive across the moor to our starting place.

At this point, I literally had no idea whether or not this would be possible. On the one hand, I do cycle a lot - I cycle everywhere! But very rarely go very far, or very fast. But as long as we stuck to our strict strategy of taking the hills steadily, and not pedalling unless completely necessary, I felt we were in with a chance.

As you might have seen, no matter what I'm doing, I tend to do it in jeans and a checked shirt - after all standards need to be maintained. But James managed to persuade me that this was one thing I wouldn't be able to achieve thus attired, so as we set off, I was already out of my comfort zone in some old football shorts and trainers [and very snazzy socks].

The route started along some nice cycle lanes and quiet roads out of Tiverton, up past the old RAF airfields, and heading towards Yelverton. To add flavour to the journey, we decided to rate the various towns we passed through on their general vibe, the availability of cake, and how fun their name was to shout in a Devon accent. Yelverton was tipped to be an early favourite, but the highly rated Dartmoor Bakery was closed, so we pressed on.

Some nice swooping roads over the moors led us towards Cornwood, and the 'how fun its name is to shout in a Devon accent' competition was put to bed early by the hamlet of Hoo Meavy.

We passed a cavalcade of motorbikers out enjoying the day, and I felt a great moment of comradery with my dual-wheeled brethren… though none of them dinged back for some reason.

Eventually we passed the chalky mountains of the Shaugh-Prior clay pits, and made the super-fast descent into Ivybridge where we grabbed an uninspiring Co-op meal deal for lunch, before taking off on a big old road-based slog towards South Brent.

Along this section we had perhaps our most exciting moment of the day, when a giant shire horse… possibly called Nathan, freaked out at the sight of our bikes coming down the road and bolted off down the road with its owner in shrieking pursuit. Shame I only caught the drama in timelapse mode, so you don't get the full terrifying sense of the incident. I'm pretty sure this wasn't our fault… I think the way we appeared out of the dark tunnel of trees might have caught old Nathan [possibly] by surprise. Nevertheless, we scooted off pretty quickly lest we face the wrath of some angry equestrians.

Anyway, we made it to Buckfastleigh and found a lovely café for a well-earnt cuppa and a photobombing from the vicar.

Day one ended with another big slog, up and down along narrow lanes towards Ashburton and Bovey where we finally had to admit we were going to have to get off and push occasionally.

We were both glad to arrive at Café 360 - a cycling themed bar in Bovey to sink a few pints of Asahi [an interesting choice for the only beer on tap] and reflect on our progress. We were 2hrs earlier than we expected, though this was mostly due to having far fewer rests than we thought we'd need. Still, the technology told us we'd been moving for 5 and a half hours and averaging 12 and a half km per hour. Look, I know it's not 'Tour de France' stuff, but we were proud of ourselves, okay?

Day 2 started with a few creaking joints, new, equally obnoxious socks, and a decision to slow it down a notch, and to stop for tea and cake more regularly.

Already, this was shaping up to be the better day of cycling, with lovely old abandoned railway lines as our main pathways, where other cyclists were out in force enjoying the flat gravelly routes. In no time we were in Mortonhampstead where we passed the world's most civil RTA, and found a place to sit in the town square for a coffee.

The next stretch was back to the undulating country lanes, and we were happy to be full of sugar and caffeine. We passed another horse, of a more manageable size this time, whose owner was clearly insane.

Next stop Chagford, a lovely looking little town, and more tea.

Next up, more slogging as we approached the steep hills of the north moor.

Perhaps the biggest surprise for me was Belstone Village, which I had assumed consisted of nothing but an army camp, but instead had a lovely green on which to sit and eat our PBJs before we realised that there was also somewhere to get proper food.

So we did what any prime athletes would and ordered some chips. Excellent they were, too. We even had a visit from the sheriff.

Full of starch, we took a cheeky shortcut to avoid Okehampton, and found ourselves back on some lovely cycle paths along the railway line, where cyclists of all ages were out enjoying the sun.

We crossed the Meldon Viaduct… which is actually more impressive to look at rather than from, and I for some reason I can't fathom, did this [girl power?].

Here, on the home stretch, with smooth tarmac under our wheels and the sun in the sky, a bit of hubris snuck in. James started cycling no hands, and I tried to get some dramatic shots using the selfie stick when there was a sudden off road section!

We had been puzzling for almost two days as to why a mountain bike had been suggested for a route that was so well surfaced, and here was our answer – the whole route was perfect for a lighter, faster road bike, but had a few kilometres of something more rugged near the end.

And this continued after Lydford where we were treated to a bit of proper off-road cycling which we might have enjoyed more had our backsides not already endured 100km of saddle.

The last section probably showcased the best of the moor, and even though our energy was sapped, we were treated with twittering Swallows, scenic views of Brentor Church and some impressive low-flying gliders before the final descent back to Tavistock.

Glowing with a sense of achievement, or possibly mild sunburn, we arrived back at where we started. I'd seen some great new places for future Dartmoor Podcast [not a podcast] episodes, and got some exercise.

Thanks for watching, and I'll see you again next time!

EASTER EGGS, GOOFS, AND EXTRA NUGGETS

- I call Tavistock 'Tiverton' at the start of the journey and this really annoys me. I know full well that it's Tavistock, and somehow managed to script, check, record, check, edit, check, and publish this video without realising.
- The little acoustic guitar progression that plays as we're cycling about is a composition of my own that I thought fitted pretty well – it's made several appearances since as a sort of 'journey theme' for the podcast*.
- The guitar riff as the bikers thunder past is - of course - Steppenwolf's *Born to be Wild*.

DARTMOOR ANAGRAMS

Oh no! James and I have got lost! If only someone hadn't scrambled up the names of these Dartmoor places along our route on the road signs!

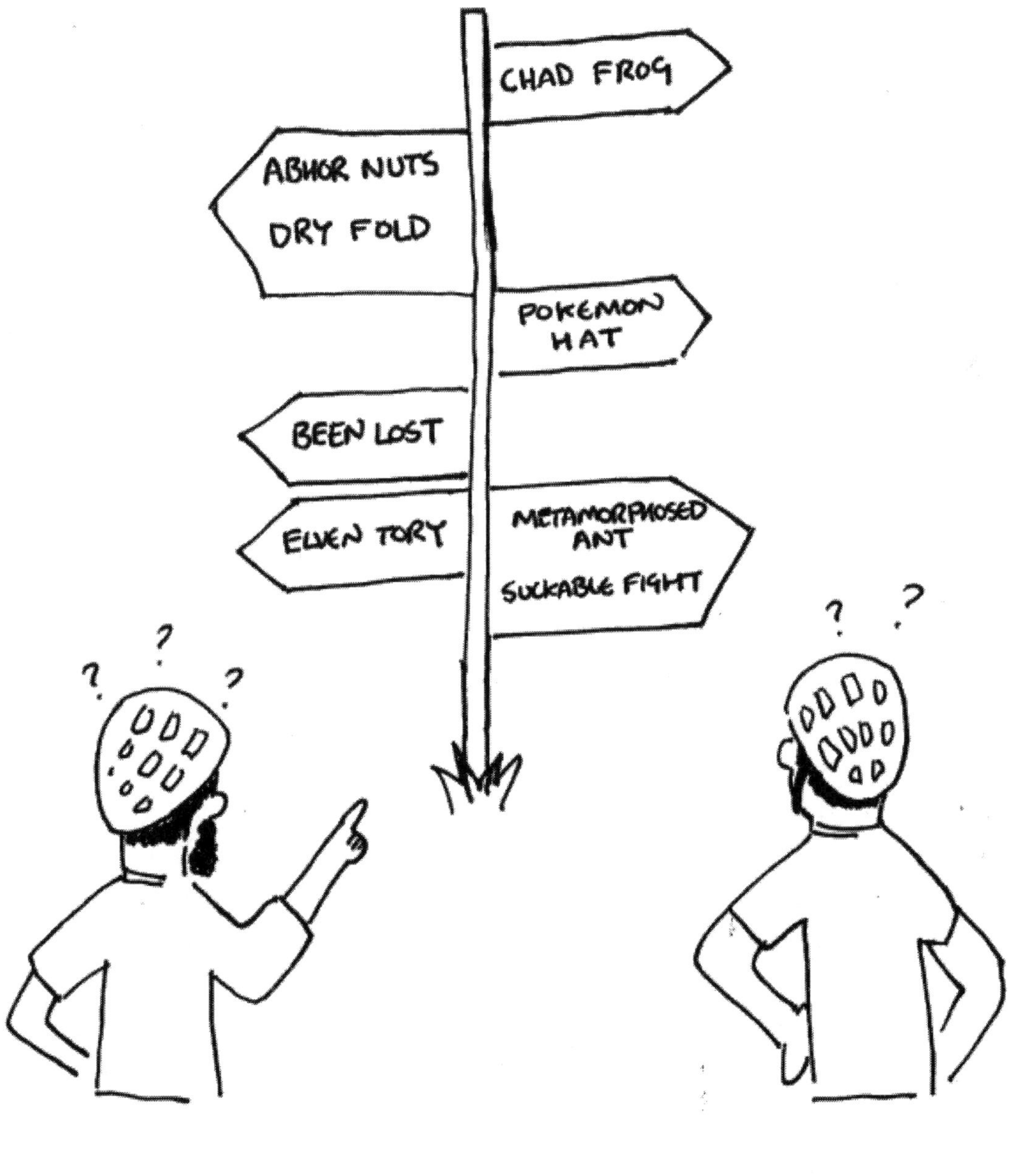

THE DARTMOOR PODCAST EPISODE EIGHT

02/10/2022

TICKS

&

MUSHROOMS

CHICKEN OF THE WOODS

EPISODE REVIEW

I like this one! I think that it could easily have been two episodes, but I manage to find enough links between foraging and acquiring Ticks that it works as a whole.

The thing I'm most proud of in this episode is just how right I got the day to film it - mushroom foraging can be quite frustrating, with seemingly good conditions yielding next to nothing, but this turned out just perfect. I have honestly never experienced such a glut of Porcinis and Parasols before or since, and certainly never so many pristine bug-free specimens.

My close encounter with the Nadder added a bit of excitement, too. It certainly set my heart racing when I realised I'd been poking about right next to her as she coiled ready to strike.

SCRIPT

Season of mists and mellow fruitfulness – there is a distinct whiff of autumn in the air, and it's easy to see why this is so many people's favourite time of year: that fine autumn light, the gentle turning of the colours, the sharp nip in the breeze, and that subtle, damp, leaf-mould aroma in the woods.

For me, autumn on Dartmoor means one thing above all - there are delicious edible mushrooms to be found!

Compared to our European counterparts, for many of whom mushroom hunting is a commonplace activity, the British seem to have an odd relationship with fungi foraging. Everyone seems terrified of them. Sure, there are a small number of species which will lead you to an agonising and uncurable death, but if you know what to look for, and don't take any risks, it's easy steer between the Scylla of liver dissolution and the Charybdis of kidney failure to reach the Troy(?) of a delicious gourmet meal.

When planning this adventure, it occurred to me that rooting about in the undergrowth for mushrooms would probably incur me picking up a few ticks, and for a while I've been thinking about learning more about these much-maligned little buggers. So, today's Podcast is a double-header. How to find and cook delicious wild mushrooms for *your* dinner, and how to avoid *becoming* dinner for Dartmoor's bloodthirsty little vampires.

Welcome back to the Dartmoor Podcast!

Mushrooms spend most of the year underground as threads of fine white mycelium which spread out under the forest floor, and weave amongst the roots of trees.

Then, when conditions are just right, they spring into existence above ground. You see, what we think of as a mushroom is really the organism's 'fruit' blooming briefly to spread its spores in the wind or via the insects that feed on it.

Which means that a mushroom, once it's opened its gills and spread its seeds, is more than happy to be picked up, shaken about, carried home and eaten.

So far, 2022 has been a terrible year for mushrooms on Dartmoor, and I expect the exceptionally hot, dry summer might be to blame. But early September saw the arrival of some rain and a cool breeze that signalled the start of autumn.

Conditions, I decided, seemed perfect, it had been dry for a couple of days, meaning my mushies wouldn't be soggy, but a midweek downpour would surely have been the catalyst to jolt them into life. Still, you can never be sure - mushrooms are as mysterious as they are wilful, and I was full of nervous anticipation as to whether I'd find any.

But as it turned out, I'd got it just right - mushrooms everywhere, of all different colours, shapes and sizes.

Here's rule one of how not to die picking mushrooms: know what you're looking for. Don't go out with a big bag and pick everything you find, then look them up later, that's a recipe for disaster. Nor should you take an ID guide out with you, as the *only* book on mushrooms is this one and it's not exactly portable.

No, you should learn two or three really delicious species in detail and then go out with them specifically in mind. My targets for the day: the porcini, the parasol and the chanterelle.

The Porcini, as we'd know it from Morrisons, also known as the Cep, Penny bun, or Boletus if you're being scientific, is one of the most prized edible mushrooms. It has a smooth, rounded tan-brown cap, and a fat white stem [stipe, if you're being pedantic], and crucially, has these spongy white or pale yellow pores instead of gills. If you find an appetizing-looking mushroom that fits this description, then there is one sure test that it isn't poisonous… all the inedible boletuses turn blue when cut into. [there are *some* edible 'blue' boletes, but this seems an unnecessary risk to me] So if yours remains fresh and white like this, you are on to a winner. I have a handy mnemonic to help me remember this rule. It goes like this.

If it goes blue, don't eat it.

A much more common problem with porcinis is that the maggots and slugs like them just as much as we do, so you have to be very lucky [or skilled] [but mostly lucky] to find them as pristine as this.

Porcinis grow in mature mixed woodland, and a good tip, is to get out early in the morning, and off the beaten track: not because more mushrooms appear here, but because there is less chance that I'll have already found and picked them.

Another good tip is to search on hillsides, ditches, and other places where the mycelium's underground strands might accidentally break the surface, causing a mushroom to appear.

And if you find some on a hillside, try traversing the hillside at around the same level – this will likely have similar vegetation, sunlight levels, temperature and drainage, so will maintain the conditions that caused your first mushrooms to surface.

That's one of the nice thing about mushrooms: when you find one, there are sure to be more nearby! ('Where are your rebel friends!').

Here's how to pick them: pull them up out of the ground, then use a knife to shave away the muck around the base. This is useful to indicate if any little stowaways have gotten into your mushroom - they leave little holes as they tunnel up through the stipe towards the mushroom head.

At this stage, I usually cut through the mushroom just to double check it's free of wormy little beasties, and I remove the pores, too, as they are another favourite hiding place. What is more, the pores can often be a bit soggy to cook. What is more, what is more, I expect that I'm helping the mushroom out, by chucking its spores around the area I found it in.

I like to carry my foraged shrooms round in a net bag, as it also facilitates this spore spreading, and it stops them getting clammy, too.

There does seem to be some debate amongst mycologists as to whether it is less damaging to the mycelium to pull a mushroom up out the ground or to cut it. The fact that this is a debate at all probably means it doesn't matter much, and I prefer to uproot whole, as it can help with identification and is pretty satisfying to boot, particularly with Porcinis.

At this point, I caught my first Ticks crawling up my jeans. And immediately, we can learn something about these little monsters. First, they only seem to 'activate' when it hits 6 degrees. The first chilly part of the morning had been completely tick free. Secondly, ticks climb upwards, and only upwards.

That's right, they don't stalk you across the woodland floor or leap down on you from the branches of tall trees, they have but one simple and effective strategy: climb up as high as they can, spit some sticky goo onto their hands, then stand like a toddler who wants a hug hoping for a sheep or deer [or you] to brush past so they can latch on and get a meal.

This simple fact about Ticks helps avoid most bites. They will always climb *up* looking for your blood, so as long as your socks are tucked over your trousers and your shirt's tucked in, they have a long way to climb until they get to anywhere biteable. And if you wear a sufficiently pale colour, you'll catch them in the act and can remove them with some judicious brushing or flicking.

Anyway, more on the Ticks later.

With a glut of Porcinis in the bag, and seemingly no Chanterelles anywhere in the woods, I decided to head for a change of habitat to pick up some Parasol mushrooms. These, for me, are the finest edible mushroom with a really pleasant flavour and 'meaty' consistency. They can get pretty large, too!

Parasols grow in a easily recognisable shape, with a long, thin, straight, hollow stipe with a 'snakeskin' pattern. And this usually has a little skirt on [the 'anulus' if you're being fancy]. The cap is broad and flat with a darker nipple in the centre, and it will be covered in dark little scraps where the outer skin has torn as it grew.

There is one look-a-likey to be wary of - the Shaggy Parasol - which is, well, shaggier, and without the snakeskin stipe. Even this is completely edible for most people, but gives some a bad tummy. On this note, anyone could be allergic to anything, so if you're eating a new mushroom for the first time, it's best to just eat a little bit.

Rummaging around in the bracken looking for Parasols was bound to get me a few new Ticks, but little did I know I was in danger of getting a much worse bite. Did you see it?

I've never met an Adder that didn't run [slither] away from me before, but this grumpy old lady was determined to stand her ground. What a beauty!

Fun etymological fact: Adders should really be called Nadders, but over the years people misheard 'A Nadder' to be 'An Adder' so often that the name changed.

I find the stipes of Parasol mushrooms a bit tough, so like to just pick the caps, which, like the Porcinis, I carry around in a net bag.

Some beautiful Sloes were out up here, too, looking pretty damn plump and glaucous. They looked good enough to pop into your mouth like a juicy Grape or Damson...

At this point I had quite a haul of mushrooms, so headed back to camp to conduct some Tick-based experiments.

There was time for one last mycological surprise, though – a beautiful Chicken of the Woods fungus growing out of this tree. This is a delicious though very unusual mushroom, which really does have a chicken-like flavour and texture. It's unmistakeable - bright orangey-yellow and growing in these large brackets out of the sides of trees. Underneath, it is white when fresh, and like the porcini, it has pores rather than gills. I helped myself to a few big chunks, and left the rest to the forest.

By this stage, the inevitable had happened and I had been bitten by a Tick. A tiny one. And the big worry with Ticks is the danger of Lyme disease - a very real and unfunny illness.

Luckily, only a small percentage of Ticks carry the disease, and even then it can mostly be avoided if you find and remove the Tick early. No need for anything fancy here, just gently tweezer the little bastards out or pick them out with your fingernails.

Over the years I've had more than my fair share of tick bites. From experience, they very rarely bite below the knee or below the elbow, instead preferring to crawl upwards and find somewhere sneakier and dingier. I've been bitten on the backs of the knees, my armpits, my beep, my beep, and round my beep. One hid out in my belly-button for several days, and once, one managed to attach itself to the tear duct on the inside of my eyelid.

Luckily, none of these bites ever developed into the distinctive red 'bullseye' rash that foretells Lyme disease. If you ever see something unusual like that around a tick bite, get it checked out, as it can be treated with antibiotics if caught early.

As it turns out, Ticks actually have a pretty interesting life cycle. An adult lays thousands of eggs which hatch into pinhead sized larvae. These usually attach themselves to a rodent or bird, have a cheeky meal, then drop off and moult into a larger 'nymph' tick which targets larger prey. If this larger tick manages to feed, then it falls off again and moults again into full grown adult about the size of a lentil.

I think that the reason I have escaped Lyme disease despite having been bitten so many times is that I tend to get bitten by the tiny 'larvae' ticks, so they probably haven't even caught it themselves yet. By being observant and wearing pale jeans, I see the adult Ticks coming and brush them off.

But was there anything else I could do to reduce Tick bites? Not surprisingly, 'DEET' an insect repellent is meant to be good at discouraging the little blighters, and perhaps more surprisingly, so is garlic.

With this in mind, I decided to attempt a bit of cowboy science to see if Ticks really could be repelled by these substances. Sorry, my lovely butterfly stag t-shirt.

I scarpered about, ridiculous human that I am, dragging this material across the forest floor to collect ticks, then treated one with a line of garlic, one with a line of DEET, and kept one as a control. As expected, the ticks all started clambering upwards as per their programming.

The ticks on the DEET treated cloth certainly seemed to stop their ascent once they reached the chemical line, and even ones quite a distance from it seemed to think better of climbing any higher. The garlic treated one had a similar, though less marked effect, while the control group just kept climbing.

It's no substitute for frequent checks and a good brush down, but it would appear that spraying a bit of deet around your ankles and waist might help reduce tick bites further.

Now, what to do with those mushrooms?

[don't make fires on Dartmoor]

Porcinis and parasols both cook beautifully in a bit of garlic oil [perfect for repulsing those ticks, too!] and marry well with a splash of soy sauce. I kind of undermined the gourmet nature of this meal by adding them to a pot noodle, but I can assure you it was absolutely excellent, especially those perfectly seared chunks of Porcini stipe which took on the consistency of a scallop or some such delicacy.

Anyway, I really enjoyed making this episode, and hope some of you might be emboldened to go and forage for some mushrooms yourself.

Just remember to know what you're looking for, tuck your trousers into your socks, apply some deet, and look out for Nadders!

See you next time.

EASTER EGGS, GOOFS, AND EXTRA NUGGETS

- The 'Scylla and Charybdis' joke sounds really clever, but actually doesn't stand up to any scrutiny whatsoever - it should be used to describe navigating between two difficult or equally bad decisions rather than just a way of talking about two bad things that could happen to you. Pedantic, I know.
- The Pheasant, Cuckoo, and Chaffinch sounds used to cover the swearing are from the 'Dawn Chorus' episode. This has become the staple way to cover bad language in the podcast*.
- This episode is filmed - you guessed it - in and around Lustleigh Cleave and up near Hunters Tor. Don't you dare use this information to steal my mushrooms.

MUSHROOMS WORDSEARCH

There are twenty species of British mushroom hidden in here. How many can you find?

N	T	B	A	D	R	E	A	R	T	H	B	A	L	L	S	P	W
L	I	I	K	S	E	O	P	C	A	T	I	E	O	I	R	O	L
G	N	K	N	S	P	A	R	A	S	O	L	C	C	Y	F	R	R
R	T	O	A	K	E	S	T	F	C	N	T	K	P	E	E	C	E
H	R	N	O	T	C	T	W	H	A	Y	E	E	L	F	R	I	H
G	K	P	N	A	Y	A	T	E	C	N	T	L	R	I	M	N	S
L	N	H	A	R	O	U	P	E	E	A	E	R	L	N	A	I	U
R	E	L	F	C	U	P	T	R	S	R	P	L	E	O	W	B	L
M	O	R	E	L	C	I	M	N	E	I	L	S	P	B	F	R	B
W	L	A	N	K	T	M	G	T	R	I	R	T	S	L	I	I	E
B	F	V	N	T	R	E	N	G	G	E	I	G	Y	S	I	L	L
C	I	E	U	G	L	A	H	E	F	W	V	A	R	A	O	E	T
H	E	M	N	F	H	R	L	U	E	T	G	I	I	E	Y	C	R
J	L	O	F	C	I	T	F	L	E	A	P	U	E	D	S	A	L
V	D	U	E	M	T	R	B	S	R	F	H	A	I	C	T	U	R
E	R	T	P	O	D	B	N	I	L	I	C	E	R	O	E	W	L
T	X	A	M	N	U	M	C	E	T	R	L	A	G	N	R	D	I
N	R	O	H	K	N	I	T	S	S	T	L	W	R	C	N	D	E

THE DARTMOOR PODCAST EPISODE NINE

27/10/2022

HALLOWEEN SPECIAL:

WISTMANS WOOD

THE FACE OF OLD CROCKERN

EPISODE REVIEW

It would be quite easy for The Dartmoor Podcast* to become some sort of ghost-hunting channel - despite not believing any of it, I do enjoy the thrill of trying to spook myself out. So I'm glad I made a promise to do just one such episode a year for Halloween - it forces me to get a bit more creative and produce more varied material.

Watching this brought back some happy memories of the recording day - it was a really nice solo adventure which was capped off perfectly by that Barn Owl. The GoPro camera I use makes everything look really tiny, so it doesn't do justice to just how close that owl was as it came to inspect my torch beam.

The sound of the ghost terrier remains a mystery, too, though there have been some good suggestions in the comments with several people suggesting it could be a Roe Deer. Anyway, it was a nice spooky note to round up the episode!

SCRIPT

Anyone familiar with Dartmoor will know that there isn't a square mile of the place that isn't roamed by some sort of ghost, devil, or spectral beastie. Either that or there'll be some curse, or legend, or harrowing tale from days of yore. And to stop my whimsical little podcast getting swamped by the supernatural, I'm trying to limit myself to one paranormal adventure per year...

Welcome to the Dartmoor Podcast Halloween special 2022! At least one spooky event guaranteed.

On a sunny Saturday in early October I found myself on a rickety bus heading towards one of Dartmoor's most, sinister, malevolent and ungodly places...

No, not the *Miniature Pony Centre*, I'm headed for somewhere densely haunted even by Dartmoor's standards: Wistmans Wood.

To start with, let's clarify my position on the paranormal: I don't believe in it. Not at all. Not even one bit. Which is why I'd actually love to experience the unearthly. I want to have my world shaken by something I can't explain. Something that would make me rethink everything and be as a child again open to the magic and mystery of the world.

So I vowed to set my scepticism aside for just one day, and go into this adventure with an open mind. After all, who knows what goes on out there amongst the granite and the oaks when no one is around to see?

The first stop on my mini ghost-tour was Crockern Tor. A very unassuming little pile of rocks right by the noisy B3212 that cuts across the middle of the moor.

Crockern Tor has a bit of real history associated with it: way back in the 14th century, it was situated right in the centre of Dartmoor's four tin mining districts, so became the meeting place for the 'Stannary Court'. For over 200 years, whenever important decisions had to be made, the tin miners would travel here across the moor to hold their meetings here in this natural amphitheatre strewn about with great granite slabs.

But as we're being Halloweeny, there is also a Dartmoor legend from this place: it is the home of Old Crockern, a bona fide Dartmoor deity, a personification of Dartmoor itself, a kind of Devon Gaia who punishes those who damage the moor. It is said that you can see the profile of his face in the stacks on the south west corner of the outcrop, but if he was there, I didn't find him...

Back to that noisy road for a moment. Perhaps one of the best-known Dartmoor legends is that of the Hairy Hands... a pair of spectral disembodied hands that appear suddenly on a car's steering wheel and swerve them off the road. And sitting on Crockern Tor and listening to the speeding motorcyclists roaring along the B3212 I was surprised that no one seems to have suggested a connection between Old Crockern and the Hairy Hands... after all he seeks to punish those who damage the moor, and building a noisy road right through his back yard would surely be enough to anger him into causing a few crashes.

Anyway, if there *is* a capricious nature spirit that punishes Dartmoor's enemies, then I think we're on pretty good terms. After all, I love Dartmoor and do my best to treat it with respect. And it certainly seemed like Old Crockern did me a favour with that map in episode 6!

I decided to make my way towards the wood slowly, seeking out a few Letterboxes en route, and taking in some of the stunning views from Littaford and Longaford Tors, crossing the ancient Lych way, an old route on which dead bodies were transported, and where, apparently, the spectres of monks make ghostly funeral processions across the moor at night.

At this point, I got my first look at Wistmans Wood, low and dark, hunched in the valley below.

It is certainly an unusual place. Woodland on Dartmoor is a rare enough commodity as it is, but this tiny copse is comprised almost entirely of Oak trees which the poor soil, boulder-strewn floor, and howling winds of the high moor have conspired to keep dwarfish and stunted, growing in a twisted tangle of spindly branches.

The etymology of Wistman is disputed, but may be derived from 'Wise man's Wood', as it is believed, by some, to be an ancient and sacred grove of the Druids... but as usual with all this Dartmoor Druidy stuff, there is no real evidence for it. These mystical looking symbols, for instance, certainly aren't thousands of year old. They are folk-art at best - vandalism at worst, as these mosses can take a very long time to grow. But we can say with near certainty that the wood has remained here a very long time, as there are the remains of Bronze age buildings all around which don't encroach into the wood itself - possibly because it was a sacred Pagan site of worship... or possibly because there are just a load of boulders everywhere making it impossible to build on or turn into farmland.

As for the age of the trees themselves, they are older than they look, but not old enough to have seen the druids. A small tree was chopped down in Victorian times and found to be 163 years old. And by calculating the size of the trunk, compared to the largest oaks, it was estimated that the oldest trees were no more than 400 years old. This little science experiment is immortalised in a carving on a rock called the Buller's Stone... which I'd forgotten to note down the exact location of, and didn't find... No, really this time!

Another possible origin for the woods' name is from the old Devon word 'Whisht' meaning eerie or haunted. And seeing that this is a Halloween episode, let's go with that.

And this word 'Whisht' also leads us to what is, on paper at least, the most menacing monsters in the area: the Whisht Hounds. A pack of demonic dogs that kennel amongst the boulders of Wistmans Wood and wake on moonlit nights to pursue lost travellers across the moor.

Perhaps the most interesting thing about the Whisht Hounds is that they are a sort of folk lore trope that appear in many northern European cultures – the 'Wild Hunt' where some deity chases the unbaptised to their doom. On Dartmoor the leader of the hunt is either our friend Old Crockern, or the big bad – the Devil himself.

As a filthy unbaptised myself should I have been worried? Well, I reasoned that if there really were a pack of hellhounds that roamed this part of the moor, and tore hikers to bloody shreds under the light of a full moon, then it might have popped up on Devon Live at some point. I wasn't concerned.

In fact, I was more freaked out by the *other* paranormal pooch of Wistmans Wood. The ghost of a small terrier called Jumbo who went missing here many years ago, and whose spirit can be glimpsed scuttling among the mossy boulders. Strangely eerie!

...And while we're talking about ghostly canines and rocks that look like things – how about this rock here that looks just like a Daschund? Anyone else see it?

What other supernatural presences could I expect to encounter if I snuck down into the valley to explore Wistmans Wood at night?

I decided to wait for evening in a state of meditation - thinking about the druids, and the wild hunt, and Old Crockern, and poor little lost Jumbo... I wanted to shake off my cynicism and be ready to experience whatever the night threw my way.

Light thickens, and the crow makes wing to the rooky wood. Good things of day begin to droop and drowse, while night's black agents to their preys do rouse.

Alright, Macbeth!

I couldn't have asked for a more perfectly creepy evening, with a bloated and sickly moon seeping through a wreath of scrappy clouds. The dark was punctuated by the glowing eyes of enormous cattle who lowed sadly in the blackness as I made my descent towards the haunted grove.

But the highlight of the trip was this. A very close visit from Britain's spookiest animal, flying right into my torch beam as I tried to get some eerie images of these rocks. A stunning Barn Owl. Anyone who has ever filmed nature with a camera and then gets home disappointed with how tiny and distant it looks will appreciate how close this beautiful creature was!

And maybe it was because I was so buzzingly happy after this experience that I didn't find the night scary at all. It was all rather beautiful – and I spent a while carefully shuffling along the woodland fringes filming the delicate and strange lichens that festooned the mossy branches of the Wistmans Oaks.

Eventually, I retreated away from the wood (where wild camping is not permitted), to get good night's sleep while leaving my camera to capture a very weird and varied time lapse of the night sky over the wood.

But there was one strange thing. Something I truly can't offer a good explanation for.

For this to make sense, I'll have to let you in on a little secret as to how this podcast is made.

Ever wonder why it sounds so gorgeous? Well, the answer is this - the Zoom HN2, a portable high-quality surround-sound recorder. And when I'm off filming things like this slug or this stick, I leave it recording somewhere out of earshot, so that if I get a great shot of a slug or a stick that is ruined by me breathing heavily or rustling about in the background, I can overdub it with the unblemished nature sounds captured by my fancy microphone. And this time, when I came to start editing, amongst my recording of the woods at night, I heard this…

Want to hear it again?

Sounds a lot like a little dog to me!

Now, I'm not saying it's the sad and wandering ghost of Jumbo … but it is creepy. I mean, could it be a fox or some other woodland mammal? I'd certainly be very surprised if there was someone walking their dog at that time of night, and I didn't see or hear anyone out there… but on the other hand, as unlikely as that explanation is, I think it's still more likely than that a spectral terrier visited my microphone while I was off filming moss.

Being open-minded works both ways, I suppose.

I headed home no closer to having my reality shattered by an interaction with the realm beyond. And I was going to do a whole bit on the psychology and biology of fear… but I just didn't get scared.

There's always next year, though! So I'd love to hear any suggestions that you have for Dartmoor places that will give me goosebumps.

Thanks very much for listening, and I'll see you next time.

EASTER EGGS, GOOFS, AND EXTRA NUGGETS

- Loads in this one, starting with the normal Dartmoor Podcast* music morphing into the spooky Saint Saens's *Danse Macabre* (or, if you're of a certain generation, the *Jonathan Creek* theme tune).
- In the intro, while sitting on the rock in the woods I take a deep breath and briefly go translucent.
- The '*Psycho*' sound effect used in the Miniature Pony Centre joke is my strumming the bits of string above the nut of my guitar.
- I made what I thought was an obvious joke about not finding Old Crockern's face, then stand up from a position where it is blatantly behind me... this went above a few people's heads.
- About halfway through, when filming the rock in the woods with my bag next to it, a ghost George peeks out from behind a tree in the background.
- The weird Doppelganger scene and the subsequent 'The Good George is in the Lodge' message is a reference to my favourite show - *Twin Peaks* and one the scariest moments in TV history.
- There's a little bonus bark thrown in at the end, then a little bonus '*Psycho*' stab, too.

THE WILD HUNT

In this episode, I mention that Old Crockern leads 'the wild hunt' through the woods on a moonlit night, and I feel this could do with a bit more unpacking...

'The Wild Hunt' is interesting in that it's such a widespread piece of folklore. There are versions in practically every northern and western European country, and each place has its own twist on the familiar theme of an unruly bunch of ghostly huntsmen chasing people through the forest. It was Jacob Grimm (of fairytale fame), who first collated a number of these stories back in 1835 and drew the connections between them.

It seems to have started in pre-Christian times, and probably in Scandinavia, with Odin as the head of the hunt. But the leader of the chaotic horde changes depending on the time and location of the story - usually it is a historical character from the region known for their cruelty.

The chasing animals have great variety, too. Sometimes the spectral riders are described as being on the backs of eight-legged horses, sometimes black goats, and the chasing 'hounds' may be werewolves, or even eagles!

As well as being pretty bad luck for the person caught by the hunt (you would be, at best, swept up in it and carried far away, or at worst sent to eternal torture in hell), it was also seen as a bad omen. Wild Hunts preceded famine, war, or an outbreak of plague.

Wistmans Wood has one of Britain's most famous Wild Hunts. It is led by either the Devil, Old Crockern, or, strangely Sir Francis Drake... I have a theory of my own about that in a future episode!

THE DARTMOOR PODCAST EPISODE TEN

08/11/2022

WILD CAMPING BAN ON DARTMOOR?

SPITE CAMPING

EPISODE REVIEW

I often say that The Dartmoor Podcast* is a sort of character I put on who is far more reasonable than the real me. I was properly angry about the camping ban, but managed to conceal my rage to put forward this much more measured assessment of the situation.

And (apart from the rap) I'm pretty pleased with it.

I think I managed to dissect a quite complicated issue into an easily digestible chunk, and I reckon I was on the money in uncovering the Darwalls' real reasons for proposed ban.

In hindsight, I was pretty perceptive, too, in spotting the exact line in the bylaws – the one about 'open-air recreation' – that would be the focus of much semantic quibbling in the court cases.

The 'rap' bit is the only thing I've done on the channel that makes me cringe. I think it was a potentially good joke, but just not well executed enough. If I were to dissect it, the problem is that you can't tell *why* it's meant to be funny - is the joke that my rapping is bad? Or that the lyrics are funny? Or just the surreal idea of there being a naughty Pony Rap Crew called the DNPA? It needed to be just one of these things to land, not all three.

SCRIPT

It's a cool, dingy and damp October morning, with heavy rain forecast for later. A terrible time to be off wild camping on Dartmoor. But I'm going anyway, because very soon, I may not be allowed to.

Normally, The Dartmoor Podcast is more interested with the events of the distant past than the present day, but for once, I'm going to poke my nose into current affairs and investigate a story that national newspapers including The Times and The Guardian have been reporting: that there is an attempt to ban wild camping on south Dartmoor.

Now, I don't normally try anything topical - firstly, because by the time I've researched, filmed and edited something together it'll probably be out of date - and secondly, because I'm an idiot who knows nothing about politics, the news, or the law.

But, if someone's going to take away my wild camping, then I want to know about it!

Welcome back to the Dartmoor Podcast.

I love wild camping. There's nothing better than heading off, alone, onto the moor with just a vague destination in your mind, and a ton of snacks in your rucksack. It's an unparalleled sense of freedom. No phone. No worrying about next week. No one to put on a face for. Just me and the sky and the moor. Give me a couple of days a month like this to wander, and think, and marvel at the beautiful landscape, and I'll be fine. I think it does me the world of good, and I know I'm not the only one.

Climbing up out of the Erme Valley, I visited Tristis Rock – a great little outcrop for the Dartmoor Hipsters who prefer their less well-known tors. In recent years, I've been really impressed with this little bit of habitat around here... the trees are naturally regenerating along the valley, and it is alive with all sorts of moorland birdlife in spring. And today, through the cloud and mist, I am able to enjoy flocks of migrating Redwings and Fieldfares shooting through from the north, signalling the beginning of winter.

And from Tristis Rock, I could look north and get a glimpse of the land that is under question.

About a decade ago a city fund manager, called Alexander Darwall, and his wife Diana bought a massive 2,784 hectare wilderness of barren hills called Stall Moor. All the land that lies between the River Erme to the east and the River Yealm to the west now belongs to the Darwalls.

Until recently I hadn't even thought about who 'owns' Dartmoor. I'd just assumed that as a national park it was sort of owned by everybody, but the land itself actually does have owners. Rich ones, with just 14 people owning about half the moor (there's a great Devon Live article called 'who owns Dartmoor' to illustrate this).

And until now, these privileged few have respected the centuries old right to camp out on the moor, making Dartmoor just about the only place in England where wild camping is legal.

And even if some of them didn't like it, they've just had to deal with it, because a byelaw in the Dartmoor Commons Act of 1985 states:

The public shall have right of access to the commons on foot or horseback for the purpose of open-air recreation and a person who uses the commons for that purpose without damaging any wall, fence, hedge or gate, or other thing ... shall not be treated as a trespasser.

Lovely.

So why is this suddenly under threat?

Well, the Darwalls claim to be 'seeking clarification' on this law. And I guess their argument hinges on whether they can claim that wild camping is somehow above and beyond the mentioned 'open-air recreation'. They say that they want a change to the rules so that people will have to 'seek the landowners consent' before camping on their land.

Which, at first, doesn't sound too much like a threat. Except that the landowners might not give consent or even be contactable at all. And then there's the greater worry that this could cascade into all sorts of other bans. If wild camping can be banned, then what about access entirely? And what about other land owners? Might they use the precedent set by this case to ban camping on their land too?

I stomped out onto Stall Moor to see what we'd be missing if the Darwalls did get their way. As, although this is a rather bleak and barren part of the moor, it's not without its points of interest.

First up, there's Hillson's House - the remains of a strange and desolate dwelling right in the middle of nowhere, with great views of the Erme valley.

Right in the middle of nowhere. Here's a problem with Stall Moor. It's actually pretty hard to get to. If you want to get out here and experience the view from Hillson's House then you will either have to commit to a very long walk... or go on a camping trip. This inaccessibility has been further confounded by the Darwalls closing the areas only car park, at New Waste, about a decade ago, so they have some previous form in preventing the common people from accessing their part of the moor.

Which is a shame, because the second point of interest here deserves more visitors. Stalldown Row. Europe's largest stone row. A mysterious north to south configuration of huge incongruous granite megaliths that stretch well over half a kilometer across this exposed hillside.

No one knows what these bronze age folk were up to thousands of years ago when they built this. But the barrows and cairns around it suggest it might be some sort of memorial. I like to think that this was the resting place of some great leader. Look how far you can see from up here, and how you can see the remains of bronze-age villages and farms on the hillsides all around. Perhaps some great king or queen of the tribes brought people together, and organised them into carving out a living here among the tors.

Now, all of this belongs to the Darwalls. And it's not just the moor. To the south, the Blatchford Estate with its large tracts of farmland, holiday cottages, pheasant shooting woods and deer park, belongs to them too.

As a man who can't even afford to buy a house, I can't get my head around the amount of money required to purchase all of this. And if you had so much space, would you really begrudge a few wild campers sneaking up here for a night under the stars?

Finally I reached Yealm Steps, a waterfall that was in good flow after all the recent rain, tumbling picturesquely over the boulders of the open moor, and running down into a little valley covered in the scars of tin mining from centuries past. Not a bad little spot to set up camp!

Now, according to the articles I read, the Darwalls are citing damage to the moor as the reason they want to put a stop to camping on their land. Is there any truth in the idea that wild campers cause damage to the moor?

Well, if we look back to the summer of 2020, at the height of the pandemic, when foreign holidays were banned, vast numbers of people who would normally have jetted off to Ibiza or wherever, descended on places like Bellever forest and Wistmans Wood, and decided to have a go at wild camping. Except, that they largely didn't do it very well. They just rolled out of their cars, popped up a cheap tent by the road, did some damage with a disposable barbeque, then drove home, often just leaving their stuff for the rangers to clear up. Pretty despicable behaviour.

But these weren't wild campers. These vandalistic grockles became known as 'fly campers', and the DNPA stepped in to sort things out, placing a temporary ban on camping in those places. The DNPA, by the way, are not some late 80s rap crew, but the Dartmoor National Park Authority.

They also addressed the 'fly camping' problem, by adding some clarification as to what actually constitutes *wild* camping: you can carry all your stuff with you, stay for one or two nights max, with fewer than six people, staying out of the sight of roads and settlements. And, crucially, you leave no impact: no litter, fires or polluting.

But the DNPA never stepped in on Stall Moor... because there was never a problem on Stall Moor. As already noted, it's hard to get to and not well-known. And furthermore, the plague of 'fly camping' has completely dropped off since 2020, because people have gone back on their cheap European holidays.

I had a thorough search for damage caused by campers on this part of the moor, and all I could find was this little area that seems to have been a fire pit at some point. Not exactly a scene of ecological devastation, and not even necessarily wild campers.

So it feels a little bit like the Darwalls are using the damage caused in Bellever back in 2020 to justify their ban on wild camping. But why?

I spent a rather damp and uncomfortable evening drying my socks on the Darwalls land (the things I'll do to prove a point.), then packing up in the morning, noting how little damage a wild camper really does.

So far, all rather odd. This isn't a wild camping hot spot, and wild campers don't cause much damage, so why are the Darwalls kicking up a fuss about it?

And it was only when I opened up a question about this to the internet, that a slightly more sinister theory emerged.

And it has to do with hunting.

I know for a fact that the Blatchford Estate breeds large numbers of pheasants to shoot. And their website offers links to deer stalking, too. And more than one person on twitter recalls seeing fox hunting on their land, though they would no doubt claim they were 'trail hunting'.

And all this jogged a distant memory of my own. About seven years ago, I was walking on their land near Piles Copse, when I bumped into two blokes in very unusual traditional garb who were walking a pack of what seemed to be otter hounds along the river. They said they were hunting mink, though whether a hound knows the difference between a mink, and an otter, I don't know.

Could it be that the Darwalls want to keep the south moor as inaccessible as possible to minimise the amount of prying eyes reporting their hunting activities?

I headed home with my wet boots, pausing briefly to empathise with some soggy ponies, and wondered how this story would play out. Hopefully, the Darwalls' legal challenge just fails and things go back to normal. I'm happy to say that quite a few people are standing against them including the DNPA, the ramblers and a bunch of environmentalist groups, too.

But what about the worst case scenario? What if their challenge, sorry, 'clarification' succeeds and a swathe of Dartmoor landowners put an end to wild camping. Well, the consensus from the wild campers seems to be 'so what?'

After all, wild camping isn't legal anywhere else in England, and we have wild camping brethren and sistren all over the country who know that it's 'legal' to camp anywhere as long as you don't get caught. As I touched on earlier, true wild campers are freedom seekers, and I don't think their anarchist tendencies are going to be curtailed by some technicality like this.

So, in confusing conclusion, the Darwalls want to ban wild camping in a place where hardly anyone goes wild camping, and the wild campers are angry that they won't be allowed to camp in a place they had no real interest in camping in, so will camp there anyway.

What do you think? Is this a real threat to our enjoyment of the moors, or is it a storm in a teacup that the national newspapers latched on to as they knew it would get people riled?

Thanks for listening! And please don't sue me.

EASTER EGGS, GOOFS, AND EXTRA NUGGETS

- The little zooms to literal piles of bullshit are entirely intentional.
- A big goof is that I got mixed up between Stalldown Stone Row and Staldon Stone Row (I wonder how!). I am filming the impressive Stalldown Stone Row, declaring that it's the longest stone row in Europe, when it is actually the far more subtle Staldon Stone Row, situated about a mile to the north, that's the long one. Glad to finally get that off my chest.
- The 'rap' is made up of the normal theme music sampled and cut up under me beat boxing and doing my worst impression of The Beastie Boys. I think part of the reason it sounds so terrible is that I was 'rapping' very quietly as not to wake my wife who was asleep upstairs. Then again, maybe it was just inherently terrible.
- ...Which maybe I realised at the time, as I cut it short, depriving the world of the extra line "We've got more flow (erm?) than the Erme in spate / If there's livestock roaming better shut that gate". Oh dear.
- The music over the 'apology' at the end is my own depressing composition – it sounds rather lovely here over the sound of a singing Wren.

LET'S GO CAMPING!

Wouldn't it be terrible if the Darwalls' attempts to stop people unobtrusively camping on their land actually resulted in *more* people going there? Here is my camping kit checklist from my journey out there. It would be awful if anyone used it to inform their own camping trip out to stall moor.

Packs:

PLCE British Army Bergen with 'Rocket Pack' attachments.

Bum-bag.

Shelter and Sleep:

Vango Banshee 200 tent.

Mountain Warehouse 3-season Sleeping Bag.

Crivit inflatable mat.

Clothing:

Lavvu.

Shemagh.

Walking boots.

Mountain Warehouse lightweight cagoule and waterproof trousers.

Shirt, Jeans, Pants, Socks, Football socks, Warm jumper, Gloves,

Cooking:

Odoland Stove containing brew kit (teabags, powdered milk, teaspoon, other condiments etc.)

Canteen (Osprey 1l)

Packed lunch, breakfast biscuits, super-noodles for dinner, snacks, more snacks.

Hip flask of whisky

Bum-bag Contents:

Head torch and spare torch.

Notebook and pencil.

OS Map and compass.

Paracord.

Penknife.

Hygiene/Aid tin (plasters, paracetamol, puritabs, 1/2toothbrush, toothpaste, hand sanitizer, tissues).

Fire-making tin (lighter, matches, strips of inner tube).

Emergency Cigar.

Plectrum (in case I need to impress anyone with my guitar playing).

Keys (to get back into my house)

Other:

Novel.

Binoculars.

Stick.

Plastic bag for rubbish.

Mobile phone (turned off, of course).

THE DARTMOOR PODCAST EPISODE ELEVEN

06/12/2022

SEARCH FOR THE DARTMOOR VOLCANO

THE SKY TIP

EPISODE REVIEW

To date, this episode was possibly the least effort of all of my videos to make (other than the kit reviews). I just filmed myself going on a nice long walk and filled in the gaps with research.

But, despite that, it's a really solid episode – perhaps one of my favourites. For me, it captures a bit of what The Dartmoor Podcast* is about - some nice views, a bit of history, and then a sudden link to something current that you weren't expecting.

So far, no lithium mines have appeared on Dartmoor, but that big weird freeport boundary does worry me.

Also, the 'willy' joke is probably my favourite silly moment in the series. I like to have my cake and eat it by saying something intellectual and pretentious, then pricking my own pomposity with something completely daft.

SCRIPT

Dartmoor can be pretty eerie place at times. Listen to this. Do you hear that? Exactly! Unsettling silence!

Is it a special landscape that needs preserving at all costs? Or a nature desert? Should these bleak hills remain a monument to the past, or should we be looking forward to exploiting the potential of this place? Just a few of the deep questions that I'll be flippantly brushing over in this - the latest episode of the Dartmoor Podcast.

Welcome back everyone.

On a sparklingly clear, cold winters day, I set out on a very long trek over the south moor. I'd been enticed by some strange features that jumped out to me when idly scrolling the satellite imagery on google maps. What was this, for instance? And this? And what about this volcano-like mound?

My first problem, if you could call it that, was that the day was just a constant array of ever-increasing beauty. I'd stop to capture some wonderous landscape in the bright, low November sun, then five minutes along the path find something even more magical and have to stop again. If I was going to make it to the Dartmoor Volcano and back before dark, I'd need to stop getting distracted.

First there were the views of the south moorland fringes, then there was this absurdly clear stream burbling along.

Then the stunning views down towards South Brent, with Three Barrows high on the hill above. Bronze age remains, like this cairn, were everywhere reminding me that these hills haven't always been so deserted. And not just in prehistory - my next unavoidable object of beauty was Spurrell's Cross, a medieval monument used by monks as a navigational aid when travelling across the moor.

Eventually, though, thank goodness, the wondrous sights died down a bit, and I was left slogging through emptiness.

Now, anyone familiar with Dartmoor will notice there is something wrong with this scene. The path is not only visible, but broad, flat and well-surfaced!

And that's because this is the remains of a railway track. And it'd lead me a long 8 miles to the Dartmoor Volcano. Let that sink in for a second. Look around. Someone went to the effort of building a steam train out to the middle of nowhere. Why? And what happened to it?

Well, the answer lies in an ill-fated attempt to mine clay from a desolate spot called Red Lake Mire right in the centre of the south moor. And the train wasn't even for transporting the clay – it was a commuter train, carrying around 100 workmen to the clay pits each morning along with coal and supplies.

This whole seemingly insane scheme was started in 1905 when two Plymouth businessmen wanted in on the clay mining industry, but were scuppered by all the obvious mining locations on the south west fringe of the moor already being purchased. China clay was big business here in the Westcountry, as the kaolin, formed from weathered granite, is of extremely good quality.

After a bit of searching and surveying, it was realised that the area around Red Lake would be capable of producing over 3 million pounds worth of China clay, and that the infrastructure needed to extract it would cost around 27 thousand pounds. Maybe this wasn't such a crazy idea after all!

But the business, imaginatively named China Clay Corporation Limited, certainly didn't have it all their own way, facing stiff local opposition to their project which meant they didn't get the railway, and subsequently the mine up and running until 1911.

With a fair few miles behind me, I began to find evidence of industry all along the path, like these pipes which used the natural slope to carry the soft clay all the way back to Ivybridge. Here and there, little concrete bridges (clayqueducts?) were made to carry the pipes over the remains of even earlier mining efforts - networks of deep, steep-sided ditches dug by the tinners of centuries past.

And there were glimpses of what was to come at Leftlake Mire, the site of a clay mine which predates the larger operation at Red Lake. The pit from which the kaolin was extracted now being a small lake, and the waste material forming this little mound next to the railway bridge.

But some of the most incongruous and unusual features were yet to come. There's something very eerie about stumbling upon the foundations of buildings all the way out here. These are the remnants of a building where the wet clay would be left to settle and dry out a bit before being piped down towards Ivybridge.

The landscape itself is so bleak here that it's hard to say it's an eyesore, but these crumbling geometric blocks of concrete and iron really have an aura of sadness around them. A failed dream. A gamble that didn't pay off.

And these ghosts of the past got me thinking about the future...

Plymouth, just visible in the distance here, is due to become a 'freeport', a new government scheme to deregulate industry in certain areas. This could, theoretically, encourage business growth with lower taxes and fewer regulations on imports. But, on the other hand, part of the appeal to those businesses will be the lack of environmental and building regulations.

And here's what's worrying me. When you look at the boundary of the proposed Plymouth freeport, it rather sneakily, no, in fact rather blatantly, stretches out from Plymouth to encompass the whole of Dartmoor National Park.

Does this mean there's a plan to open up to moor to development and industry again? I'm sure it's no coincidence that Dartmoor has recently been found to hold large quantities of lithium, a rare element used in the manufacture of batteries, right at the time when the world is attempting to shift towards electric vehicles.

Anyway, look at these weird old structures, apparently used to separate sand and grit from the mined clay. Don't they look like giant sarcophaguses... sarcophagi? Sarcophopodes? Whatever. All of this in just about the most inaccessible and desolate place it could be. It's even hidden in the crease of the map.

And from here, finally, a glimpse of the Dartmoor Volcano. A huge pile of waste material from the mining process at Red Lake itself. This pile was called the 'sky tip', which is, perhaps impossibly, an even cooler than the Dartmoor Volcano. Look at it looming out of the landscape like mount doom over there.

As you get closer, though, you realise that, though large, it isn't quite as impressive a size as it looks from a distance. One of those strange Dartmoor optical illusions where distance and scale and perspective all get warped by the Pixies.

Sadly for China Clay Corporation Limited the Great War put a dampener on their schemes almost as soon as it got going. And even after the war had ended, it was found that the clay from here wasn't of quite as good a quality as they'd hoped. The business limped on until 1932 when it closed for good.

In time, everything of value, including the trains were sold as scrap, and the army demolished everything else.

Amazing, though, to think that this was once a bustling place. Workers would arrive on the train, and extract clay from this now flooded pit by blasting it with hoses. There was a canteen, and a bunkhouse, offices, a blacksmiths, and an engine room powering the winches that hauled wagons full of waste material to the top of the sky tip.

And that's where I'm headed. It would be remiss of me to trek all the way out here and not have a look at the view from the top.

Nothing beside remains. Round the decay

Of that colossal Wreck, boundless and bare

The lone and level sands stretch far away.

Hey, don't those reservoirs look like a willy!

A bit more poking about, then it was time for the long return walk to civilisation. If only there were some sort of train to take me back.

Thanks for watching everyone. If you know more than me (which wouldn't take much) about the 'freeport' proposals, or lithium mining, and what this might mean for Dartmoor, let me know in the comments.

Thanks again, and see you next time.

MISSING TRAIN TRACK

The old Puffing Billy track has been washed away! Can you help George find the correct route to the Dartmoor Volcano by placing the correct number of track pieces in the correct squares?

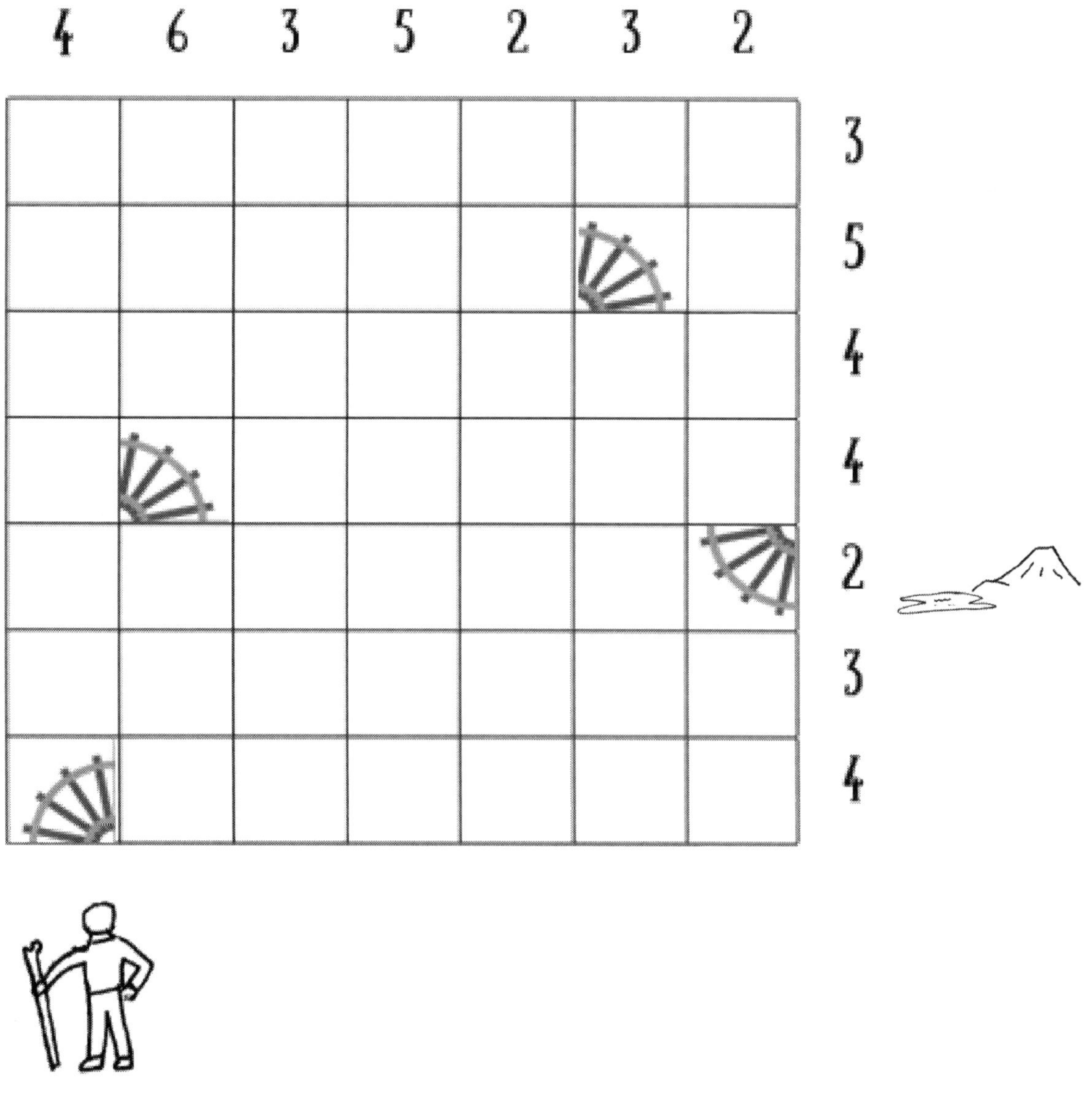

EASTER EGGS, GOOFS, AND EXTRA NUGGETS

- The music as I'm discussing 'Puffing Billy' is me playing *Last of the Steam Powered Trains* by The Kinks off their amazing *Village Green Preservation Society* album.
- Before I notice a lake shaped like a willy, I am quoting the last two lines of *Ozymandias* by Percy Shelley. A particularly apt poem that's, partly, about how mankind's endeavours are always destroyed by time and nature in the end.

THE DARTMOOR PODCAST EPISODE TWELVE

27/12/2022

WINTER THRUSHES

PSYCHO!

EPISODE REVIEW

In contrast to the previous episode, this was almost certainly the hardest episode to make. I honestly think this is my best episode in concept, but have some regrets about how it turned out - an over-ambitious first foray into nature photography included!

On the bad side, it's a bit quiet - especially that poem at the end. But in terms of script and presentation, this is really close to what I set out to achieve when I first thought of making my own podcast*.

Hardy's poem is absolutely one of my favourites, and (without wanting to get too literature teacher-y) the episode mirrors the poem in the introduction of bleak surroundings and a depressing tone before leaving on an uplifting message of hope for the future.

SCRIPT

I leant upon a coppice gate
When Frost was spectre-grey,
And Winter's dregs made desolate
The weakening eye of day.
The tangled bine-stems scored the sky
Like strings of broken lyres,
And all mankind that haunted nigh
Had sought their household fires.

The land's sharp features seemed to be
The Century's corpse outleant,
His crypt the cloudy canopy,
The wind his death-lament.
The ancient pulse of germ and birth
Was shrunken hard and dry,
And every spirit upon earth
Seemed fervourless as I.

Hello everyone!

That was the beginning of Thomas Hardy's poem, *The Darkling Thrush* written in winter 1899 - the booming Victorian age had come to an end, modern science was stripping the world of its faith, the powers in

Europe were beginning to build great weapons of war, and the new century was trundling bleakly in.

And at the end of 2022, it's hard not to feel a little bleak myself. The world is still readjusting after the pandemic, there's the cost of living crisis, the media stoking an imaginary culture war, an actual war in Ukraine, strikes, fear of climate breakdown, government corruption scandals, people trying to ban my wild camping, and the mullet is coming back into style.

So here at the solstice, let's see if we can't escape all of that, and find some solace in nature.

There is a second half to that Thomas Hardy verse, by the way, where the 'Darkling Thrush' of the title begins to sing, and if I can find a such a bird to accompany me, I'd love to finish the poem. Do Song Thrushes really sing at this bleak time of year, as the sky grows dimpsy, and when all other birds are silent?

There's only one sure way to find out… And it's going to be chilly.

Welcome back to *The Dartmoor Podcast.*

In mid-December, Dartmoor's woods are a very peaceful place. A far cry from the cacophony of spring - and on a day like today, there's no sound other than the soft falling of the last of the leaves.

But I was hoping there was still some life to be found. Especially as, on top of my usual equipment, I'd brought a bridge camera which would allow me to get some close-up nature shots like this…

Look out Attenborough, I'm coming for you.

...Or maybe not.

I'm fully aware that I'm not bringing you cinematic excellence with this, but I think it's good enough to finally show you what I can see through my binoculars.

Anyway, before too long, a sound lead me to a flock of small garrulous birds roving around, searching for food among the twigs. There is safety in numbers, so they use their sharp, insistent little calls to keep contact with the group as they work their way through the branches.

On the ground, Blackbirds, a species of Thrush, rustled among the dry leaves looking for invertebrates to snack on. And as I went stomping clumsily through the forest, I inevitably ended up scaring quite a few, causing them to shoot off, low and fast, with that familiar 'pink pink pink' call.

Sometimes I wonder that if I really loved nature so much, I'd stay at home and stop bothering it.

Now, the reason that I'm setting off so many Blackbird alarms today is simply because there are more of them about than normal. You see, as icy as it is here, it's even icier up in Scandinavia, and many millions of birds from there make the journey over to Britain for a milder winter.

And with them, come Redwings - another species of Thrush. But ones that you'll only find here in the colder months, when they migrate over here in great flocks to feast on our Rowan or Holly berries.

Here's a piece of information that will enrich your life greatly. Hear that thin, 'siip' sound? That's the call of a Redwing, and one they make frequently while migrating at night. If you keep your ears open on a cold evening, you might hear this sound as flocks of them fly above you unseen in the darkness.

So, birds call to warn each other of danger, or to keep contact with the flock when feeding or on migration... But what about bird song?

Well, this is used for a less cooperative end. It is to claim their territory and warn others of the same species to go and find their own patch. And outside of the breeding season, most birds don't bother, as singing takes up a lot of energy that could be spent actually searching for food or staying warm. Because when it comes down to it, the life of a wild animal is a mathematical balancing act of calories in vs calories out.

But a few species do sing through the winter - the payoff of having your own territory full of food is sometimes worth the initial energy expenditure. Most notably, our festive favourite the Robin sings all year long. And they are ferocious defenders of territory, happily blinding, maiming, or killing other Robins to keep their space for themselves. And they look so cute, too. *Who's a little psycho, then? Who's a little psychopath?*

And here's another winter singer – the Dipper. A most unusual bird that looks like a little like a Christmas Pudding. The Dipper, although clearly a songbird, rather akin to a large Robin, actually dives into fast rushing streams to catch insect underwater.

All rather wonderful, but I still hadn't found my main star. A singing Song Thrush. And without wanting this to get overly 'meta' and become a podcast about making a podcast, I was beginning to worry. My episode wouldn't come together without this particular singing bird. I was three very cold camping trips into December and had heard nothing more than this brief snatch of song up on Hunter's Tor. It was becoming obsessive.

Perhaps you can just about hear from this snippet the quality of a Song Thrush's erm... song. Loud and clear. Not particularly musical. But distinctive, especially in the way it repeats each phrase two or three times. I always think they sound in some way 'tropical', like something you'd hear coming from the dense canopy of a rainforest.

Other than listening carefully and keeping my eyes open, I had one more strategy for finding a Song Thrush - looking out for Thrush anvils. Song Thrushes love to eat snails, and they have evolved a trick to get through their shells, and that is to batter them against a rock. A thrush will use the same rock to brain all of its molluscs and that's why a stone surrounded by snail shells is a good sign that a bird holds territory nearby. The best example of this I've ever heard was from Twitter, where a chap called Richard Broughton found an old glass beer bottle in the woods among a huge pile of shell fragments. The bottle was dated 1954, so it's possible that generations of Thrushes had been battering snails to death in the same spot for over half a century.

Kind of feels like a depressing metaphor for something.

Talking metaphors, in *The Darkling Thrush*, Hardy uses the singing Song Thrush as a metaphor for hope. It lets loose its rapturous singing when everything else seems dead. It is a reminder that everything in nature and life is a cycle, and that the good times will return.

So, in a way, not finding the singing Thrush for my silly little YouTube video took on a deep significance for me. If I couldn't find it, it meant, symbolically, there was no hope.

In theory, finding a Song Thrush shouldn't be that difficult. It's a relatively common bird which really does sing on winters' evenings.

It defends its territory all through the Winter because it knows things will get better – the frozen, barren land will become useful again.

The winter is temporary.

A recession is temporary.

Depression is temporary.

Of course, I found one in the end, didn't I?

So please, just as the thrush repeats himself, indulge me if you would in a second, and this time complete, performance of Hardy's poem:

[Recital of *'The Darkling Thrush'*]

So, from The Dartmoor Podcast, I would like to wish all of you a very sincere 'Happy New Year'. Thanks so much for listening. Let's make 2023 a good one.

EASTER EGGS, GOOFS, AND EXTRA NUGGETS

- This is the first episode where I get a bit artsy with the colour grading. It's super subtle, but the colour is just a little bit washed out until the end when the Song Thrush sings and I bring the saturation back up. Just one of those things that no one will notice, but might just register subconsciously.
- I genuinely went on three separate camping trips to gather the necessary footage for this one. The coldest was a camp in Lustleigh Cleave where it went down to -4 in the night, hence the naughty fire for survival purposes.
- I actually get quite a few bits of the last stanza of the poem wrong in my recital, but, hey, it's near as dammit.

POEM ANALYSIS: THE DARKLING THRUSH

Probably my favourite poem of all time. Working to memorise a poem, like I did for this episode, really makes you over think things…

I leant upon a coppice gate
When Frost was spectre-grey,
And Winter's dregs made desolate
The weakening eye of day.
The tangled bine-stems scored the sky
Like strings of broken lyres,
And all mankind that haunted nigh
Had sought their household fires.

The land's sharp features seemed to be
The Century's corpse outleant,
His crypt the cloudy canopy,
The wind his death-lament.
The ancient pulse of germ and birth
Was shrunken hard and dry,
And every spirit upon earth

Note the death imagery in the first stanza – 'spectre, weakening, broken, haunted'. It's bleak!

The simile 'strings of broken lyres' foreshadows the thrush's music later on! Also,the *sounds* of the words. The 's's really stand out, and this sibilance creates a hushed 'spooky' atmosphere.

The death imagery continues in stanza two, and there's a repetitive, pulsing iambic rhythm building that mirrors the

Seemed fervourless as I.
At once a voice arose among
The bleak twigs overhead
In a full-hearted evensong
Of joy illimited;
An aged thrush, frail, gaunt, and small,
In blast-beruffled plume,
Had chosen thus to fling his soul
Upon the growing gloom.

So little cause for carolings
Of such ecstatic sound
Was written on terrestrial things
Afar or nigh around,
That I could think there trembled through
His happy good-night air
Some blessed Hope, whereof he knew
And I was unaware.

'pulse of germ and birth'.

And then it bursts into life. The rhythm is derailed slightly, taking us out of the drudgery. And that made-up word – 'illimited' – is just wonderful.

The sounds, too, are magic. The fricatives in 'thus' and 'fling' emphasise the power of the song.

'Ecstatic' here is another perfect word – clipped and rapturous.

And then the last stanza brings meaning out of the whole experience. And what a great meaning – that everything is a cycle, the wheel will turn, and hope is alive.

THE KIT REVIEWS

THE LAVVU

03/07/2022

THE LUDWIG

17/08/2022

THE BRITISH ARMY BERGEN

23/11/2022

ONWARD, HOBBITS!

KIT REVIEW REVIEWS

The idea for these stems from my frustration at how bad most kit reviews are on YouTube. There - I've said it. They are usually fifteen minutes or more long, with someone standing in their garage slowly pointing out all the zips on a coat. And you can't even trust their opinion because they were sent it for free and have only worn it once.

Okay - rant over.

I've lumped these three videos together, as, honestly, I don't really care about these videos as much as my 'proper' podcast* episodes...

A view that clearly isn't shared by the Americans. The British Army Bergen video accounts for over a quarter of my views, mostly by our transatlantic cousins, and outstrips all my interesting stuff about birds, mysteries, and rocks by about twenty times. Sigh.

That said - it's not about the views. And I do enjoy making these quick throwaway videos.

I think I'm able to get plenty of humour into these videos because I've genuinely spent two or more years alone in the woods with the items I'm talking about. This means I've had just about every silly thought imaginable associated with them.

One thing I don't understand, though, is that most people who comment on these videos seem to already own the items I'm reviewing, rather than being people scouting the kit out before a purchase... This seems very odd to me! Oh - and some of these people get quite cross if your opinion is different to theirs. Welcome to the internet, I suppose!

LAVVU SCRIPT

Hello!

Trying out something a bit new today. As a large part of my Podcast involves me wild camping up on beautiful Dartmoor, I thought I'd start reviewing some of the equipment I use on my adventures. But to make things a little different, I am only going to review items that have survived at least two years… that seems like enough time to really get to know a piece of kit, and it also means any of those things which seem great, but break after a couple of outings, don't get any ill-deserved praise from me.

Anyway, today, I'm going to talk about something that I take with me everywhere on the moors, and that you'll have seen strapped to my terrible backpack if you've ever watched any of my incredibly niche videos about rocks or fairies or whatever.

That item is the Lavvu.

The Lavvu is the Polish version of a piece of outmoded military equipment called a 'shelter-half'. Basically, a big waterproof cape. And you can pick them up pretty cheap from army-surplus websites, usually about £30 quid, but often cheaper if you buy two. That's because if you get two of them, you can sort of button them together to make a shit tent (hence the name shelter-*half*). It's way too small for two people and has no groundsheet, so I don't recommend it for this purpose

As you can see it's made of really tough canvas, and has some nice chunky buttons. The whole thing lets off an air of trustworthy durability. They have their production date stamped on the inside, so you can see that this one was made in 1976! That's right, this thing is older than me, and was probably stashed away on a shelf in some Polish depot for decades before I picked it up...

And then showed it absolutely no respect by putting it through four years of constant wild camping abuse. Abuse which it has just brushed off. It's an absolute trooper.

So, so far, it's cheap and durable. All good.

Here's the first downside: it weighs a ton. Like a lot of old army-surplus stuff, comfort wasn't really a consideration, so if you're into expensive light-weight modern innovations then this isn't for you. However, if your spirit animal is a Dartmoor Pony, and you don't mind steadily lumbering around with a bit of extra weight, then this might be right in your wheelhouse.

Like a lot of good wild camping equipment, the Lavvu is a multi-purpose item. It's most common use is as a kind of invincible picnic blanket that you can hurl down onto any old piece of ground or rock and instantly have a relatively dry and clean place to sit. This is especially useful when wild swimming and wanting a tick-free place to stand when you're getting dry.

It also makes a really good groundsheet or extra blanket for camping in cooler weather. Something about the weight and texture of it is very comforting and reassuring. It even smells kind of nice.

And of course, it's a coat. Ideal for hunkering down and sitting out a really heavy downpour. Or, because it's huge you can throw it over yourself and your backpack, so it's a rucksack liner, too.

Pull the string on the inside of the cape and tie a knot so you have a bit of shape for your shoulders, then it's just a case of buttoning it around the neck and it's done. You can keep your arms inside, or unbutton the flaps and poke them out.

You can use it to collect firewood. Then you can use it to protect that wood (or whatever else you please) by chucking it on top.

I've even heard that you can make a boat out of it… but that might be a step too far.

So I think it's adaptability makes up for its heaviness. I figure that if I took a camping stool, a thick waterproof coat, and a bigger sleeping bag instead of the Lavvu, then the weight might not be much different anyway.

The only other downside, of course, is that it looks stupid. Like you're LARPing *Lord of the Rings* or something. But who's there to see you?

A quick recap then. Pro's: it's cheap, adaptable and durable. Con's: it's heavy and embarrassing.

For me, it's an absolute essential. Making this little video showed me how much use it gets and how well it stands up to the demands of a wild camping trip. Just pick it up, shake it off and it's ready to go again.

But hey, I'm open minded! I'm so enamoured with the Polish Lavvu, that I've never even thought of trying another country's take on the shelter-half, but maybe you have. Leave a comment if you think there's an even better option out there.

Thanks for watching!

LUDWIG SCRIPT

Welcome back to another 2 year kit review.

Here I review bits of hiking and wild camping kit that have survived at least 2 years of use, so that I don't end up promoting something that seems good, but then falls apart when you need it most.

Today I'm looking at a piece of kit that you'll have seen on my back if you've watched any of my dorky videos about Pixies, or Woodpeckers or gold, or whatever.

It's a Norwegian alpine army surplus rucksack, affectionately known as 'The Ludwig', and sometimes known as the 'Telemark', because it was in some old war film or other. which

Anyway, the Northmen used it for *years*. Seriously, it was designed in *1909*, and only went out of use relatively recently!

And I have no idea why, because it's a *terrible* rucksack. An absolute nightmare.

It's heavy as hell, with no waist support, and a pair of simple leather straps which will start cutting into your shoulders in no time if you have any real weight in the pack. And most of the weight comes from this metal frame which does, to be fair, keep your back nice and cool, but also wangs into your hip every time you put it on.

It's got one huge central section that swallows your kit, and two huge side pockets which are a bit too small for any useful big stuff, and a bit too big for any useful small stuff. It has a little zippy section in the top that is too small for anything, and hard to get to…

Hard to get to…

Hard to get to…

Here's the real thing that makes this pack a nightmare. The stupid little buckles. Everywhere, sissy, fiddly little buckles. Packed up, ready to go? Oh, wait, you've left your canteen out! Ah! And I'll need my map.

God knows how the Norwegian military put up with it.

"Anders! Anders! Quickly, it's the enemy!"

"Yes, Jan, I am trying, it is these tiny buckles that are slowing me"

"Anders, we are needing more ammunition now!"

"Ah! It is in the other side."

"Where are we from Anders? This accent is very confusing"

"Buckles!"

So, I know what you're thinking. George, if it's such a terrible rucksack why are you using it?

Well look at it! It's pretty damn gorgeous isn't it?

And it's not all bad. It's cheap and it's really tough. I've battered this poor thing around for about three years now and it has never let me down.

A unique feature I really like is that you can poke stuff like an axe or a walking stick [I love my stick] down the sides. [more tiny buckles, though!].

And you can add these extra straps [even more tiny buckles!!] to the top to carry your Lavvu around, which I love. [See my Lavvu review].

I've solved the issue of no small side pouch by clipping my bum-bag round the top, too, so that negates one of the bag's big failings.

Quick recap:

Pros: it's cheap, durable, capacious, and looks great.

Cons: it's heavy, uncomfortable, has no useful small compartment, and it's fiddly.

I've sort of fallen in love with it because I've grown used to it, and developed my own little system to get around its foibles.

But, in all honesty, I'd think carefully before buying a Ludwig.

BERGEN SCRIPT

Hello, I'm George and I don't look after stuff.

If something survives 2 years or more in my care, then it probably deserves a review, and that's the tenuous premise of these videos.

Today I'm talking about an absolute army surplus classic. The British army PLCE Bergen. PLCE stands for personal load carrying equipment, which is a fancy way of saying 'rucksack'.

Let's get straight to the point. It's huge! Perhaps too huge.

It has an enormous main pouch, big enough to contain, let's say, a springer spaniel, two surprisingly capacious side pouches which could house a sturdy pug each, a large top section… miniature dachshund? And another pocket on the front here probably only big enough for a teacup chihuahua. So that's dum dum two pugs and a dum duuum, hey! About an alsatian in total.

Look, here's what I got in there today with room to spare:

My Lavvu, a stick, stove, third draft of a novel, map, mushroom foraging bag, pen, canteen, filming stuff, binoculars, dinner, notebook, snacks, whisky, waterproofs, hat and scarf, gloves, bum bag, takeaway curry, sleeping bag, bivvy bag, hammock, and a tarp, oh, and some salt and pepper sachets I'd been looking for.

Massive.

Gigantic.

Humungous.

It forces you to rethink the whole act of packing your bag. No need to compress every item into little stuff-sacks and employ tetris grand-master levels of tessellation. Just haphazardly chuck everything in there. It's very liberating.

And it's tough as hell, too. Made of really durable material in a very rough and ready kind of way. Perfect for performing the cassowary manoeuvre. The cassowary manoeuvre. You've heard of the cassowary manoeuvre right? Oh, well, when you come across dense undergrowth you can tackle it in the usual undignified manner... or you can use the cassowary manoeuvre. I mean that's also pretty undignified, but it's quicker and more fun.

Let's look at some features in more detail. Look at those chunky zips – they are never failing, and never getting caught on anything. Super! You've got some nice solid clips too (no silly little buckles here!), and a few draw string thingies if you need them. The straps are padded... though not the most comfortable in the world. And there's some padding here, too, though no frame to keep it off your back, so you can end up a bit sweaty. And there's a waist clip that doesn't actually take any of the weight onto your hips, so is a little bit pointless.

There was a very basic removable aluminium frame to keep it rigid in here, too, but it broke, so I took it out and it hasn't made much difference.

Pretty standard army-surplus stuff. It's built to be cheaply produced, functional and durable, but not necessarily ergonomic. Because soldiers are tough, right? They don't need to be comfy! They wouldn't want to be comfy! Offer them comfort and they'd laugh.

Talking army-surplus, In the lid here you've got the date it was made... mine was made at the start of the last good decade. And I've got some faded names here, too: Cox, Veal, and Milan. Your brave sacrifice shall not be forgotten. Only kidding - I'm sure they're fine.

But the British army Bergen has a cool little surprise for us. The side compartments zip off, and can be attached to this to create a really quirky little rucksack affectionately known as the 'rocket pack'!

A great idea in theory, but I have a few qualms.

For starters, this would be much cleverer if it could be constructed out of the actual straps of the main pack rather than having to carry this extra 'yoke' around too. And secondly, because once you've removed the side pouches, you've already created a smaller, lighter pack by... well, removing the side pouches.

Still - it's three back packs for the price of one, which shouldn't be scoffed at!

Also, there is a reason why this bifurcated design isn't frequently used in backpack manufacture, and that's that you can never remember which side you put the thing you needed in.

Nonetheless, I quite like the rocket pack. It's comfy, light, and unique. And sometimes when you're on a long march and you feel a bit jaded and tired out, you remember it's called the rocket pack and that's enough to make you smile and give you a little boost.

The bergen isn't waterproof, but that's not a problem as you can just stick a bin bag in there. I say it's not waterproof, but it's suspiciously good at keeping water *in* once it's become inundated which is sod's law, I suppose.

Should I sum it up?

Positives:

It's big, it's tough, and it's adaptable.

Negatives:

It's cumbersome and pretty uncomfortable.

In conclusion, it might not be pretty or fancy, but when the inevitable zombie apocalypse occurs, this is the bag I'll be taking with me.

Thanks for listening!

EASTER EGGS, GOOFS, AND EXTRA NUGGETS

- The little guitar noodle at the start used as a 'kit review theme' is my cover of either *Girl from the North Country* or *Boots of Spanish Leather* by Bob Dylan. How can it be either? He plays the same guitar bit for both, as far as I can tell!
- The Lavvu and Bergen videos are filmed in... you guessed it – Lustleigh Cleave! And the Ludwig episode was filmed as I was making the Sherberton Stream episode along the Dart.
- If you look closely, I have a black eye in the Lavvu review. I'm usually sporting some sort of injury from playing football, and they are usually my own fault for throwing myself around the midfield into people much bigger than me.
- I really was carrying the third draft of an unfinished novel around in the Bergen review. It's about a boy and his enormous dog becoming accidentally entangled in an international spying situation and escaping by running away across – you guessed it – Dartmoor! It's still not finished. Probably because I'm procrastinating by writing this instead.

APPENDICES

A lot of planning goes into making an episode of The Dartmoor Podcast*. Well, normally. The less work I put in the more people watch it, seems to be a rule!

Anyway, here are some pages of notes etc. that show just how chaotic and random the process is. Most are from my little notebook, but many are scrawled on the back of bits of paper from when I've been bored at work.

"Search for Cranmere Pool"
CRANMERE POOL
Est. 1887
DARTMOOR
AUTUMN
MYTHS & FACTS
HOW NOT TO DIE
MUSH-ROOMS
BIOLOGY
TICKS
LYMES DISEASE
FORAGING

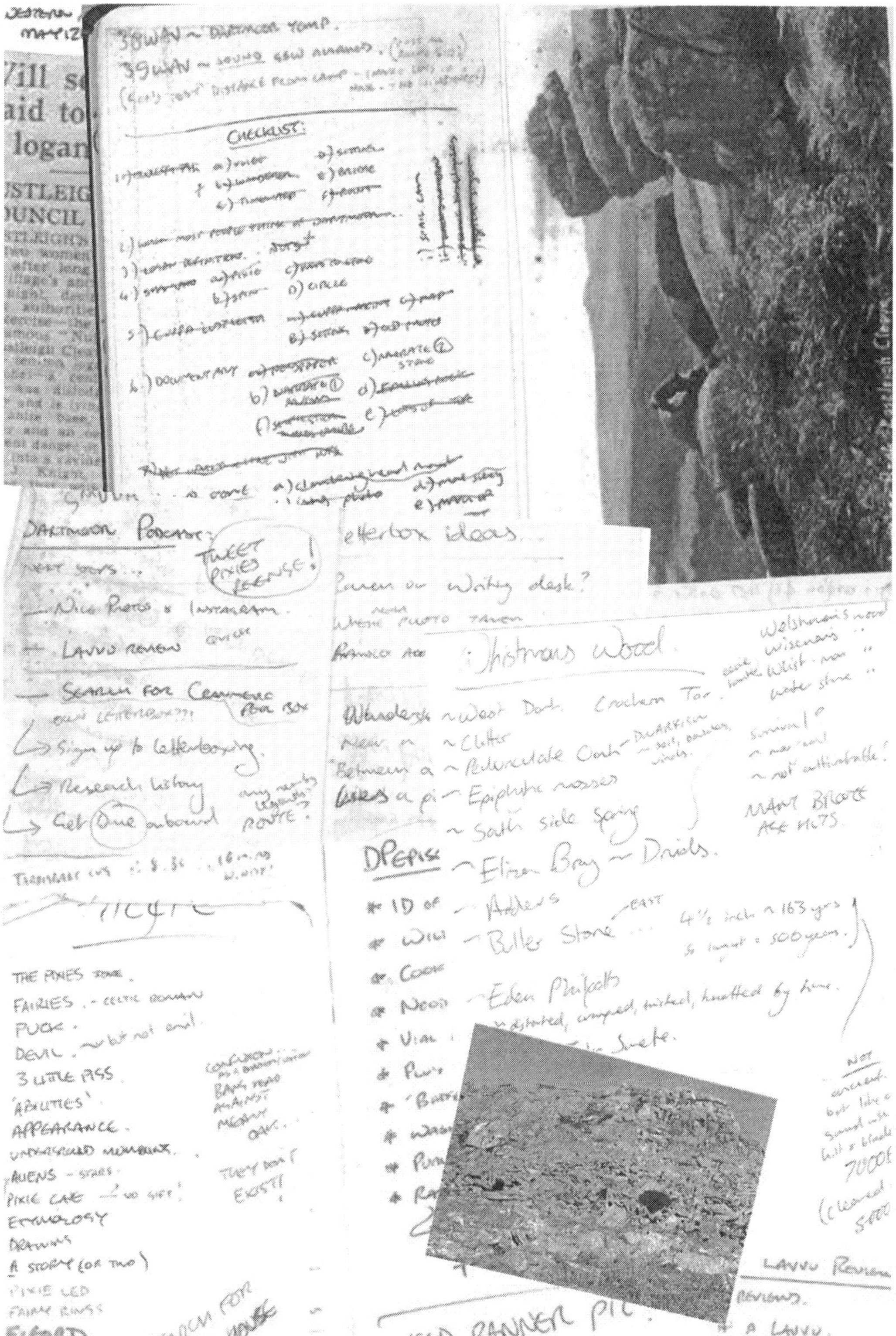
CHECKLIST:
DARTMOOR PODCAST:
TWEET PIXIES LICENSE!
Letterbox ideas...
Camera or Writing desk?
Sign up to letterboxing.
Research history
Get One onboard
Wistmans Wood
~ West Dart. Crockern Tor.
~ Clitter
~ Pedunculate Oak
~ Epiphytic mosses
~ South side Spring
~ Eliza Bray ~ Druids.
~ Adders
~ Buller Stone
~ Eden Phillpotts
THE PIXIES TOME.
FAIRIES
PUCK.
DEVIL
3 LITTLE PIGS
'ABILITIES'
APPEARANCE.
ALIENS
ETYMOLOGY
A STORY (OR TWO)
PIXIE LED
FAIRY RINGS
ELFORD
NEED BANNER PIC.
LAVVU REVIEW

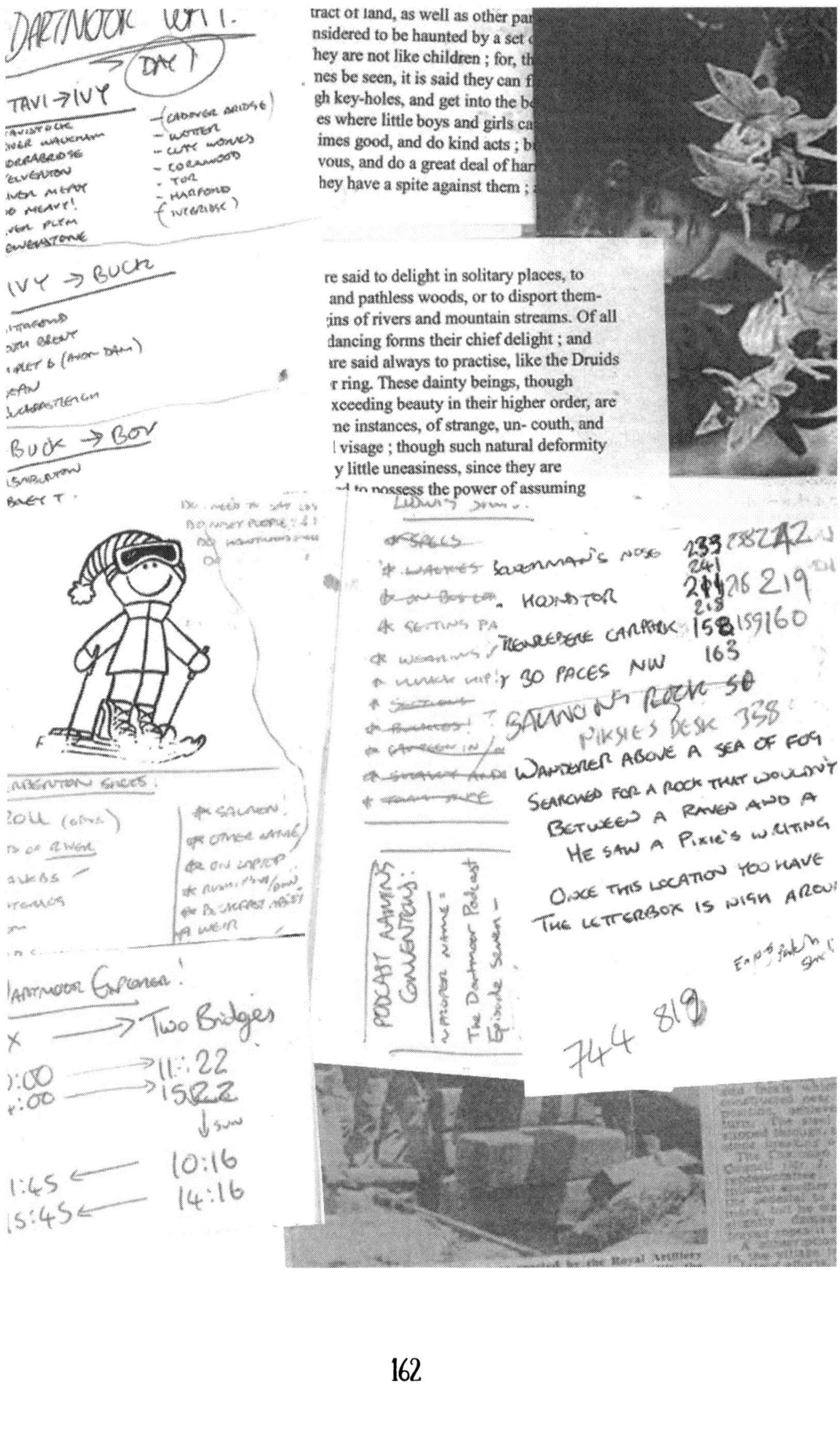
tract of land, as well as other pa
nsidered to be haunted by a set
hey are not like children ; for, th
nes be seen, it is said they can f
gh key-holes, and get into the b
es where little boys and girls ca
imes good, and do kind acts ; b
vous, and do a great deal of har
hey have a spite against them ;
re said to delight in solitary places, to
and pathless woods, or to disport them-
gins of rivers and mountain streams. Of all
dancing forms their chief delight ; and
are said always to practise, like the Druids
r ring. These dainty beings, though
xceeding beauty in their higher order, are
ne instances, of strange, un- couth, and
l visage ; though such natural deformity
y little uneasiness, since they are
d to possess the power of assuming
DAY 1
TAVI → IVY
IVY → BUCK
BUCK → BOV
HOUNDTOR
30 PACES NW
PIKSIE'S DESK
WANDERER ABOVE A SEA OF FOG
SEARCHED FOR A ROCK THAT WOULDN'T
BETWEEN A RAVEN AND A
HE SAW A PIXIE'S WRITING
ONCE THIS LOCATION YOU HAVE
THE LETTERBOX IS NIGH AROU
PODCAST NAMING CONVENTIONS:
Two Bridges
11:22
15:22
10:16
14:16
744 819

SATURDAY 6th.
Cooking mushies.
— test night settings for Halloween.
— BROLL! WALKIES! BASSIES!
SMOKES, GARLIC, DEET
TICK IMPRESSION
DIFFERENT TICK STAGES?
~ PONIES / SHEEP / DEER
ROOTS
LEAF LITTER
SMELLING
EIIR
TQ13 88
DAWN CHORUS.
START 1:40 ish.
2:30?
ROBIN 2:40
WREN 2:50
CUCKOO! 5:00
BLUE TIT 3:30
BLACKCAP
BLACKBIRD
CHAFFINCH 10:10
PLANE STOPS
CHAFFINCH
BTIT
CHAFF
100 hour
BLACKCAP
STLEIGH
ROCK'
ndals' with
of upsettir
The people who live in these humble dwellings are not very nice, for the pig-stye is generally near the door, and the children are not much cleaner than the pigs. It is the more discreditable to their mothers to let them be so, as there is water enough around to wash and keep clean all the children in Devonshire.

SPECIAL LINK

Would you like access to some bonus footage? Sadly, there isn't too much from 2022 as I didn't really think to keep it… but there are some bits and bobs that people might find amusing.

If you'd like access to the 2022 extra bits, then email me at thedartmoorpodcast@gmail.com with the code word 'Illimited', and I'll send you the link!

PUZZLE SOLUTIONS

FOXES YARD

HARTON CHEST

OLD CLAM BRIDGE

RAVENS TOR

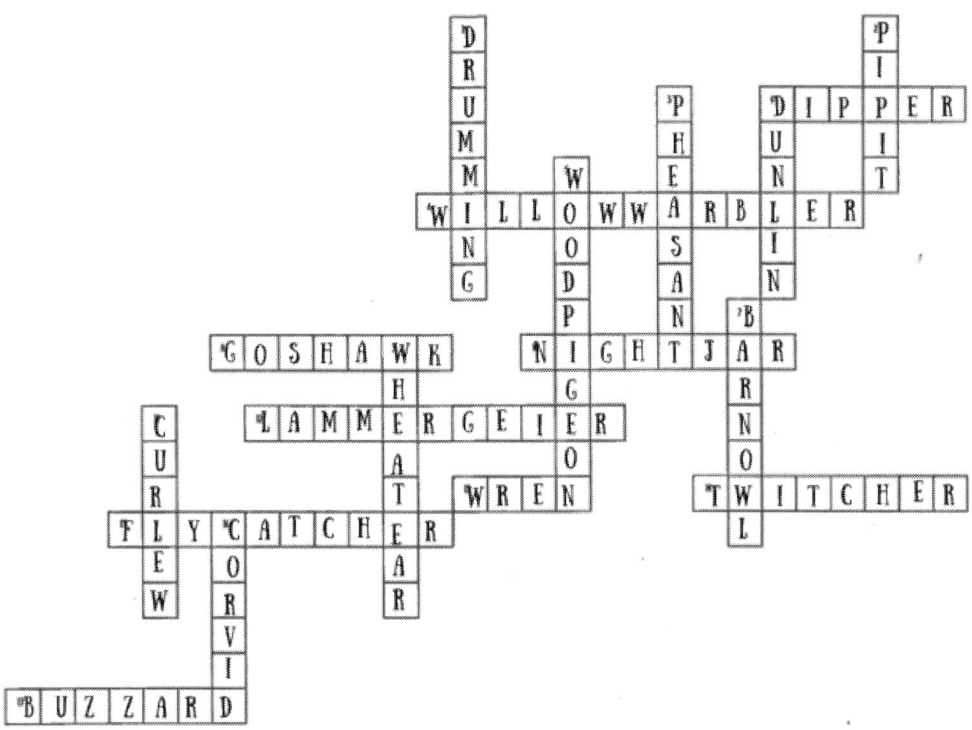

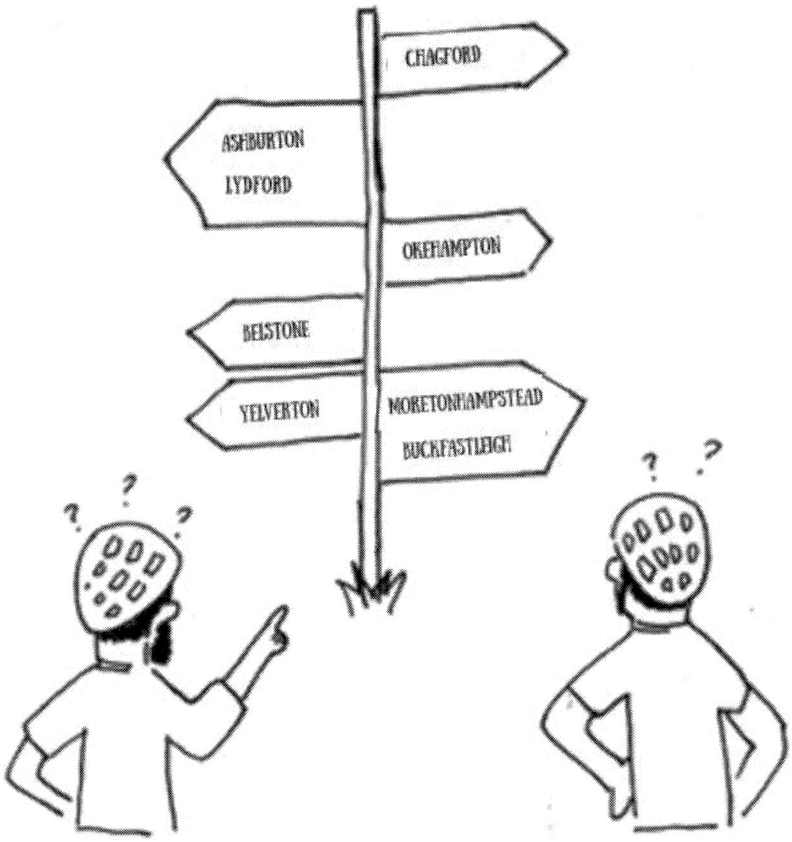

N	T	B	A	D	R	E	A	R	T	H	B	A	L	L	S	P	W
L	I	I	K	S	E	O	P	C	A	T	I	E	O	I	R	O	L
G	N	K	K	S	P	A	R	A	S	O	L	C	C	Y	F	R	R
R	T	O	A	K	E	S	T	F	C	N	T	K	P	E	E	C	E
H	R	N	O	T	C	T	W	H	A	Y	E	E	L	F	R	I	H
G	K	P	N	A	Y	A	T	E	C	N	T	I	R	I	M	N	S
L	N	H	A	R	O	U	P	E	E	A	E	R	L	N	A	I	U
R	E	L	F	C	U	P	T	R	S	R	P	L	E	O	W	B	L
M	O	R	E	L	C	I	M	N	E	I	L	S	P	B	F	R	B
W	L	A	N	K	T	M	G	T	R	I	R	T	S	L	I	I	E
B	F	V	N	T	R	E	N	G	G	E	I	G	Y	S	I	L	L
C	I	E	U	G	L	A	H	E	F	W	V	A	R	A	O	E	T
H	E	M	N	F	H	R	L	U	E	T	G	I	I	E	Y	C	R
J	L	O	F	C	I	T	F	L	E	A	P	U	E	D	S	A	L
V	D	U	E	M	T	R	B	S	R	F	H	A	I	C	T	U	R
E	R	T	P	O	D	B	N	I	L	I	C	E	R	O	E	W	L
T	X	A	M	N	U	M	C	E	T	R	L	A	G	N	R	D	I
N	R	O	H	K	N	I	T	S	S	T	L	W	R	C	N	D	E

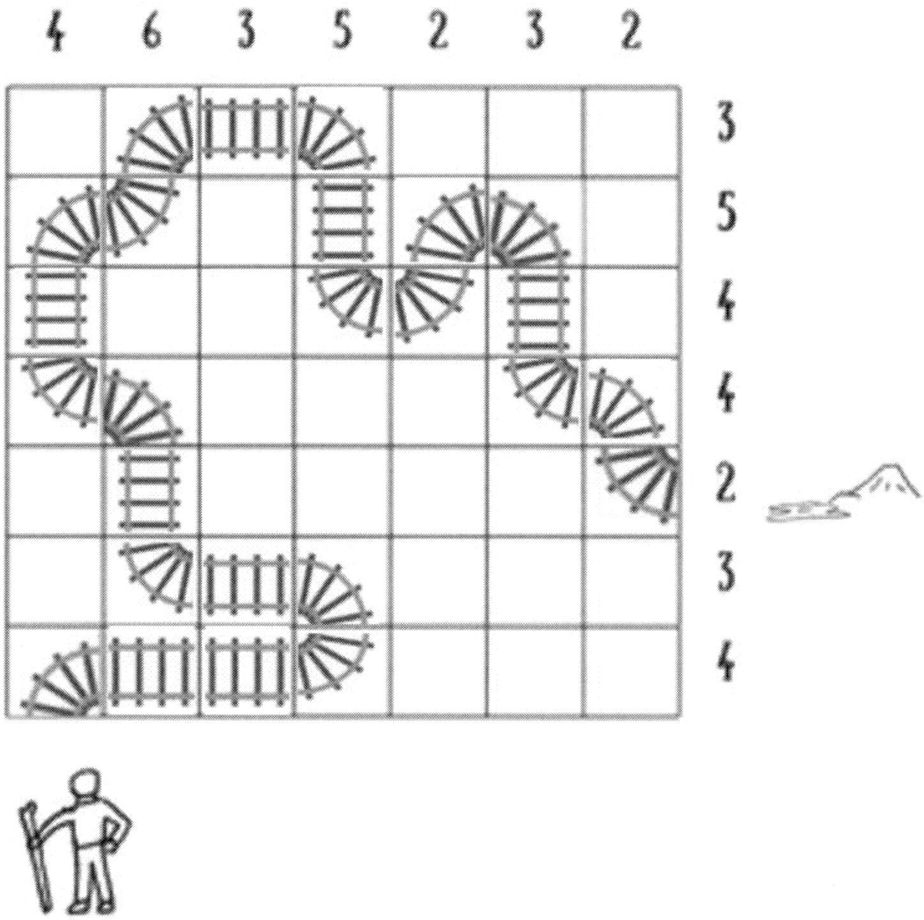
4 6 3 5 2 3 2
3
5
4
4
2
3
4

Thanks again for buying The Dartmoor Podcast* Annual 2022. It means a lot to me that people watch my silly channel. And remember,

*It's not a podcast